D1246781

The Biggest Moonshiner

Betty M. Rafter

PAGE PUBLISHING, INC.
New York, NY

First originally published by Page Publishing, Inc. 2019

ISBN 978-1-64544-859-4 (Paperback)
ISBN 978-1-64628-128-2 (Hardcover)
ISBN 978-1-64544-860-0 (Digital)

Printed in the United States of America

I was inspired to tell our story to honor our parents and my siblings, especially our oldest sister Dink, to whom I dedicate this book.

Chapter 1

We choose our fate with the choices we make.
—Gloria Estefan, song title

The Great Depression was starting to wind down in 1939, but not for us. On a frigid morning in Sopchoppy, Florida, ten days before Christmas, Mama, Daddy, my two older sisters, my two older brothers, our baby sister, and I were hiding out in a shack deep in the woods of the Apalachicola National Forest, south of Tallahassee. Daddy said we were on a fun adventure, but my oldest sister, Dink, said we were on the lam, running from the Feds.

My sister Lois, almost two years older than me at five, and I sat in homemade chairs pulled up close to a red-hot woodstove in the middle of a one-room tar paper shack, playing. "Okay, my turn," she said. "What color am *I* imagining?" Our oldest sister, Dink, twelve, walked behind us with year-old Baby Bright Eyes bundled in her arms, singing "Rock-a-bye Baby." My older brothers Robert and Mack, ten and eight, argued quietly about whose turn it was to bring in firewood from the frozen pile outside. A small pine tree in the corner, as far away from the stove as the parameters of the small room allowed, was draped with homemade strings of popcorn, dried red berries from the woods out back, and faded thin glass balls dangling on scant branches. There were no gifts beneath it.

Mama and Daddy were sitting across the room on a bench by the long, heavy homemade wooden table. She sighed and shrugged her shoulders. "Urbie, we are almost out of groceries." She nodded toward the little Christmas tree, adding urgently, "I need to do some shopping!"

He said, "We can't take a chance on you going into town, Shorty." That's what he called Mama because she was only four foot eleven. "You may get recognized. Make a list of what you want, and I'll get someone to do the shopping when I go to Jacksonville."

She scooted closer to Daddy and took a deep breath. She appeared to be explaining something else to him. Her fingers were tracing circles on the table as they spoke quietly.

He said, "Don't worry, Shorty! As long as the kids are in the car, they'll never suspect anything around here."

"But, Urbie, I'm afraid they will...with the jugs...what if...they catch us?"

He slammed his fist on the table. I almost jumped out of my chair, and we all froze when he said in a booming voice, "Damn it, Leila! I don't like it either, but we gotta do whatever it takes to put food on this table for you and these kids." He only called her, or any of us, by our real names when he was angry—which was seldom.

Mama took a deep breath, pushed up from the table and put the jam away, wiped the crumbs from the table, and threw them into the fire. She took the baby from Dink's arms and said softly, "You and Robert fold the quilts and put the mattresses against the wall, and we'll take your daddy to work."

I didn't want to leave the shack. With a roof over our heads and a floor under our feet, we were living in a mansion, after more than a year in abandoned houses with leaky roofs and no windows, or else in our army tent down by the river. Why, Daddy barely got our shack closed in before the onslaught of winter. A stack of rough slabs of lumber to cover the thick tar paper on the outside was stacked in an icy pile behind the shack, but it was warm inside. I was happy we no longer had to worry about the tent leaking when we touched the canvas or huddle around a fire outside or tuck ourselves under quilts in our straw beds to keep warm.

Mama bundled Baby Bright Eyes tighter. "Mack, put a couple more pieces of wood in the stove to keep the fire going until we get back."

We all put on our coats, and Daddy swatted Mama on the bottom as she got to the door.

We piled into Daddy's shiny new black V8 Ford. As we drove away from our shack, down the winding and bumpy dirt road, through the woods, Daddy started singing "Little Brown Jug," and we all joined in. "Log broke through, and I fell in—but I hung on to my bottle of gin…"

"Urbie, I wish you wouldn't teach the kids songs about that stuff. There are a lot of other good songs to sing."

"Okay, what do you want to sing, some of your church songs?" Those were the only songs she was allowed to sing growing up in an evangelical home. She didn't answer him.

He started, "Row, row, row your boat…" We kids joined him, singing in rounds.

As we turned onto the gravel road that led to the Ochlocknee River, Daddy hit the gas pedal. The car jerked, accelerating faster and faster. Mama, with Baby Bright Eyes in her arms, braced herself against the door and asked him to slow down. The trees became less distinct as we flew past them. Laughing, he turned toward my snickering brothers in the back seat and waggled his finger. "You know, boys, this hot rod can outrun anything in Wakulla County—not like our old truck."

As we approached the sharp curve in the road on two wheels, Mama pleaded, "Urbie, please slow down." She held the baby closer, as I slid against her. He slowed the car and turned south onto a narrow path that meandered along the side of the river's edge. The path was barely wide enough for the tires to avoid an occasional dip off the track onto the hard packed, muddy beach. Daddy dipped in and out of the water to tease Mama and thrill us kids. The sun was just coming up across the water, casting streaks of blazing orange and gold through the pines and illuminating the towheads piled in the back seat. We were laughing, enjoying the bouncy ride over the ruts and roots of the tall pine trees and magnificent hundred-year-old live oaks that formed a canopy overhead.

Following a dirt road overgrown with weeds, we suddenly took a sharp turn through a thicket of high brush that scraped both sides of the car and closed behind us.

Jip Jones, who lived in a shanty nearby, was already there. He had been working with Daddy since we left Alabama. We met him while picking cotton and hiding out near Dothan in the abandoned house where Baby Bright Eyes was born. Daddy asked him to join us and work for him. We left Alabama for Biloxi, where Daddy planned to truck farm, but we left there suddenly and somehow ended up in our tent by the river in Sopchoppy.

Robert waved to him. "Mornin', Jip Jones."

Daddy's moonshine still

He looked up and nodded, still shoveling. "How's dem chil'ren today? Mornin', Mista Urb and Missus Leila." He shoveled something from a barrel into a large copper container that looked like an oversize woodstove and added a piece of wood to the fire. A long, skinny, twisted copper pipe was connected to the top and extended into a wooden barrel with a tap at the bottom.

Jugs filled with clear liquid waited under the tree where Daddy parked by his old work truck with the fake floor in the back. Empty jugs sat on the ground behind the big stove. We stayed in the car while Jip Jones, Daddy, and Robert loaded the filled jugs of liquid into the trunk of the car. Mama handed the baby to Dink and walked around to the driver's side. She stood on tiptoes as she hung on to the open door and looked nervously in all directions. We lifted our feet as they loaded more jugs onto the front and back floorboards. Mama took a slow, deep breath as Daddy loaded the last jugs and covered them with an army blanket. Robert climbed over the jugs and closed the door, and Mama slid under the steering wheel. As he patted the front fender, Daddy told Mama, "We'll come home for dinner around noon." She nodded and slowly backed the car through the brush-covered opening, her gaze continually sweeping in all directions, as she drove back through the woods. She looked relieved as she parked the car close to the porch of the shack and turned off the engine.

Dink and Robert helped Mama unload the jugs while the rest of us went inside. Between the three of them, they shoved the heavy table and benches off the big flowered rug, rolled the rug back, and pulled up the hinged hatch that opened into Daddy's tar paper–lined dirt cellar. They carefully maneuvered the steep ladder as they transferred one jug at a time into the cellar and placed them next to the ones already there. When all the jugs were moved, they closed the hatch and put everything back in place. Mama exhaled.

Dinnertime came and went, and Daddy and Jip Jones had not come home for dinner. We were getting hungry, smelling Mama's vegetable-beef soup, rice, and cornbread. Mack, who was always hungry, pleaded, "Mama, we're 'bout to starve to death. Can't we eat?"

She reluctantly served our plates but didn't sit or eat with us. She covered two generous servings with clean dishcloths and put them on the elevated warmer rack on the stove, then paced around the shack, glancing out the window at the dirt road. After we finished eating, she told Dink, "I'll do the dishes while you get the baby down for a nap. Robert, get some wood chopped and have Mack help you bring firewood in for the night. The temps are supposed to get down to near freezing."

She did the dishes and put them away on the shelves above the kerosene summer stove and kerosene lamps. She checked the five-gallon cans to see how much was left of her stock of dried beans, rice, flour, cornmeal, and lard. After folding diapers, she started helping Mack with his reading, while Dink and Robert worked on their multiplication tables. Mama was a good student. She graduated from ninth grade tops in her class, before she married Daddy at fifteen. She often said that learning to read and to do multiplication tables wasn't all there was to education—that we needed to be in school with others our age.

Mama put a chunk of fat back into a pot with the turnip greens Daddy brought home yesterday. She seemed to be somewhat in a daze as she took two jars of blackberries from the shelf, usually saved for special occasions, and made a cobbler. She waited later than usual before she made cornbread and fried pork chops from the box of salt in the corner, to go with the turnips for dinner. We were all beginning to sense Mama was worried, so we didn't nag her about eating. The time for our traditional gathering around the stove had passed by the time we finished supper, but Mama said, "Why don't you eat your cobbler around the stove before you sing."

After eating dessert by the stove, we started our traditional singing after dinner—clinking spoons, plucking our homemade gut bucket, and strumming thimbles up and down Mama's brass washboard, as we sang silly songs and hymns. Singing wasn't the same without Daddy playing the mandolin. Mama usually joined in, but after she washed the dishes, she sat quietly, rocked Baby Bright Eyes, and hummed along when we sang hymns.

We stayed up way past our bedtime before Mama told us to go to bed. Dink and Robert pulled the mattresses onto the floor and distributed the quilts. After we said prayers, asking God to bring Daddy home safe, I asked, "Mama, When *will* Daddy be home?"

She bit her lip and said, "That old truck probably broke down. He should be home anytime now."

We eventually went to sleep for the night, except Mama, who hardly slept at all.

Chapter 2

Sorrow looks back, Worry looks around, Faith looks up.

—Ralph Waldo Emerson

Mama heard the putter of an engine approaching our shack at dawn. She jumped up and grabbed her house coat, rushing toward the door. As she pulled the quilt that covered the window aside, she heard the knock. "Leila, it's Vester."

She recognized the voice of Daddy's youngest brother. She opened the door and saw him standing there holding his felt Stetson cowboy hat. Her heart almost stopped—for him to drive from the Glades in the middle of the night meant bad news. She didn't move.

"I hate to tell you this, Leila. Urbie got a message to me, so I could let you know what happened—"

She interrupted, "He sent a message—so, he's okay!" Suddenly she realized they were standing in the cold. In a choked voice, she said, "Sorry. Come in and warm up by the stove."

Uncle Vester stepped inside. "Well, he is in trouble—the... uh...Feds from Biloxi caught him delivering a load of shine, but he would have been in much more trouble if they knew he operated the still the moonshine came from. They may have had a warrant for his arrest, because they took him to the federal pen in Atlanta.

By then we were all awake, listening from the mattresses on the floor. Mama asked, "Does Jesse McKnight or Coy Rushing know about this?"

"I don't think Coy and Jesse can help, Leila. He was caught in Wakulla County—by the Feds from Biloxi. I guess they had been on his tail for a while. He doesn't have the local law on his side. They don't know him here like they do in the Glades."

Coy was brother-in-law to Uncle Jesse, Mama's brother-in-law. They were involved in politics and well-known, influential guys around Panama City in Bay County—but not Wakulla.

Mama's chest rose and fell, her lips a grim slash. Uncle Vester knew something was coming. "Didn't I tell you and Urbie to quit while you were still ahead and the kids still had their daddies?"

He knew her well enough to avoid triggering her rarely shown temper. He said, "I don't like it one bit either, that my brother's in the pen, Leila." Looking down, rolling the brim of his hat in his hands, he blurted, "Urbie was safe in the Glades! Then he followed you up here when you left him to stay with your mama and daddy." Mama blinked back tears but said nothing. He continued, "He built that grocery store and house for you in Millville and tried, but with this damn Depression, a man don't have no choice. If you don't know the hypocrites in these dry counties, you're in real trouble."

Mama bit her lip and stared at the floor. Uncle Vester put his hat on, nodded goodbye to us, and said, "Leila, let me know if I can do anything for you and the kids." We heard his truck drive away.

Mama collapsed onto the bench and rested her chin on clasped hands as she closed her eyes as if in prayer. After a few moments, she stood up straight, poured herself a cup of leftover coffee, and pulled the rocking chair closer to the stove. She said, "Now, you kids go back to bed, because breakfast won't be ready for a while." Gripping the cup, she rocked and sipped the cold coffee. We went back to our beds but didn't sleep. Afraid to ask Mama, we whispered to each other. Lois asked Dink, "What are they going to do to Daddy? Is he coming home?"

Mack asked, "What if he doesn't come home? What are we going to do?" We knew something bad was happening, and we were scared.

I remember hearing Daddy say the lawmen in the Glades didn't like highfalutin lawmen from Miami or the Coast invading their territory, so they covered for their own—and he *was* one of their own. He said, among many in the Glades, even the infamous John Ashley of the John Ashley Gang was once considered a folk hero. To them, his gang represented a partner in resisting bankers, lawmen, and the wealthy, and the Ashleys were considered good people who helped their neighbors.

We had heard Daddy tell of how, when he arrived in Okeechobee in early 1924, John Ashley's family was the biggest producer of moonshine in South and Central Florida. He and the locals were angered when Sheriff Bob Baker ambushed and killed John and his gang on November 1 of that year. He said the Baker family had occupied the Palm Beach County Sheriff's Office since 1908. When John Ashley fell out of favor with them, the slaughter of John Ashley's daddy Joe and John's gang left the people in the Glades itching for revenge—and moonshine business up for grabs.

People in the Glades were left jobless, homeless, and destitute when the Depression came early there after the Land Bust in 1925, Miami Hurricane in 1927, and Okeechobee Hurricane in 1928. Daddy was not one to give in to hard times. When selling alligator and otter hides, fish, and frog legs couldn't support his family, he said, "There's one thing that people will buy in good times and bad—in good times to celebrate and in bad times to kill their pain." He set out to make the best shine in the state. By 1929, he was allegedly "the biggest moonshiner" on the East Coast. His problems *did* begin when he left his safe haven in the Glades.

Palm Beach Post (West Palm Beach, Florida) · Wed, Oct 30, 1929 · Pag

ALLEGED "BIGGEST MOONSHINER" PLACED UNDER $2,500 BOND

Okeechobee City Man, Alleged By Dry Chief to Be Largest Manufacturer, Held Under Heavy Surety for Appearance in Federal Court

URBBIE E. MEEKS of Okeechobee City, characterized by C. H. Parks, chief of the dry bass here, as the largest manufacturer of moonshine liquor on the East Coast, and who was arrested Monday, was placed under $2,500 bond Tuesday by United States Commissioner Clarence W. Johnston. William V. Meeley, arrested at the same time by Chief Parks and his officers, was put under $500 bond.

Each was charged with sale and possession of intoxicating liquor. Information was filed against Urbbie Meeks by customs patrol inspectors charging him with conspiracy connected with the transportation of alleged liquor at Port Mayabka on the St. Lucie canal north of Canal Point.

Mrs. Ida Castle, alias Mrs. Ida Walker, arrested last week in an automobile in front of 764 South Dixie Highway after a successful raid had been made at the building, was slumbered Tuesday by Commissioner Johnston.

Nicholas C. Jones, driver of the automobile in which Mrs. Castle was passenger and alleged operator of the establishment, was placed under charges of manufacture, sale and possession of liquor and maintaining a common nuisance. Bond for Walter Symanett, negro, alleged brewmaster, was set at $1,000.

At the final hearing of Russell D. Meyers, arrested last week, bond was set at $750 on charges of sale and possession of liquor.

new road from 760 feet to

After breakfast, Dink, Robert, Mama, and Mack were doing multiplication tables, when Jip Jones's rusty old jalopy clunked into the yard. Mama quickly stepped outside. We followed, but she told us to go back in. We went inside, but we could still hear their voices through the tar paper walls.

Jip Jones's voice shook. "Is der something wrong, Missus Leila? Is Mista Urb sick?"

"Bad news, Jip Jones. Urbie got caught, and he's in jail in Atlanta. I'm praying Coy can get him out, but I don't know this time."

"I'm sorry ta hear dis, Ms. Leila. Why they wanna to go locking up a good man like Mista Urb, when he's just trying ta make a living fo his family in hard times?"

Mama said, "I know, I know, but there's a lot of people doing things we don't want to be doing to get by."

"Yes, ma'am, that's der truth."

Robert, Mack, Lois, and I watched through the window. He added, "They's a drop of good luck, Missus Leila. Mista Urb was driving that ole truck, and they didn't take yo new car."

Robert, listening, turned to Mack. "Yeah, but if Daddy had been in his new car, they couldn't catch him."

Mama said, "He was probably turned in by a local bootlegger who wasn't happy about him invading their territory. This whole thing can get real nasty."

"Ah know, ah know, Missus Leila. What we gonna do now?"

"The first thing to do is destroy every trace of that still. If they learn he has a still, they'll put him *under* the jail."

"Ah hope Mr. Urb won't get mad about that, but ah will. Ah'll haul it away today."

"I don't care how angry he gets—if they find these jugs in his shack, they'll put him away permanently. He's got to get rid of them when he gets out, and we'll take these kids home and get them back in school. There's got to be a better way."

As we sat by the window listening, Dink was busy taking care of Baby Bright Eyes, and suddenly realized we were hearing too much. She quickly dropped the quilt over the window from the nail to block our view. By then we were all scared. She said, "Yes! Daddy's coming home!" She softened her voice. "It's going to be okay, so go play in the back of the room."

When Jip Jones left and Mama came in, Robert asked, "Mama, what are we gonna do? Are we going to Granny's?" He especially loved to go to Granny's. The last time we were there, Mama didn't want him using the ax, but Granny said he was plenty old enough to chop wood. He knew Mama never disputed anything Granny said. Mama said, "No, Robert, we have to wait here until Daddy gets back."

Mama cooked dinner in a daze, trying to think of what she should do next. Mack burst through the front door, yelling, "What's for dinner, Mama?" She hardly realized the food was ready. We finished eating, the dishes were done, and Mama was sweeping when Grandpa's big logging truck pulled up. She rushed out to meet him, very glad but not surprised. Grandpa had come to take her and the kids to safer ground years earlier.

He'd come to get her from the Glades when he and Uncle Vester were bootlegging in Canal Point. He took her, Dink, Robert, and Mack back to live with him and Granny. The same midwife, Cindy, who had delivered Mama twenty-five years earlier delivered Lois in Granny's feather bed two weeks after they arrived. That was before Granny and Grandpa divorced and he moved to Charleston.

Mama, like Granny, was petite, under five feet tall. She was a beautiful olive-skinned girl, alive with spirit, with intense eyes that reflected wisdom beyond her years. She inherited dark-brown eyes, high cheekbones, and long, thick black hair from Grandpa Wester's great-grandma, who was a full-blooded Cherokee. Mama was the oldest of six siblings—the only one without auburn, red, or strawberry-blond hair or blue eyes, like Granny's Dutch Irish family. She adored her daddy and was more like him than like Granny.

James Robert Wester was a quiet, hardworking man, well-liked by everyone he met. He looked for the best in people and didn't believe the hell and damnation he heard from the pulpit of Granny's church. Mama, like him, felt uncomfortable with some of the sermons, but she loved to sing more than anything in the world. She and her siblings would walk to church with Granny every Monday and Wednesday evening and on Sundays, where she would sing as

Granny played the piano. Grandpa didn't attend church except on some occasions when Mama sang.

Mama could plant a garden, can the harvest, cook, sew, clean, do laundry, and care for children as efficiently as any good home-maker. Granny believed idle hands did the work of the devil—and she made sure no one around her had idle hands.

Mama lived a quiet and busy life with her parents and siblings in their modest home. She had only known the peaceful but strict lifestyle of Granny's evangelical Baptist upbringing in her little hometown in the Panhandle of North Florida. The occupants there were paper mill workers, local small-business owners, and preachers from the many little churches in their close community. Their livelihoods depended on enduring the pungent odor from swirling clouds of smoke that billowed from the stacks above the paper mill and filled nostrils for miles. All activities were associated with work and church, which created a sort of "same old, same old" existence that caused the younger generation to be anxious to leave—and in their later years, even more anxious to return.

Grandpa wrapped his arm across Mama's shoulders, hugged her, and extended both arms in a group hug as we rushed to meet him. He asked, "Are you and the kids alright, Leila? Your mama sent me to get you, and I came as soon as I could." Though Grandpa and Granny had parted ways back in 1935, Grandpa was always there when the family needed him.

Mama said, "It's good to see you, Daddy, but we're fine. I'm sure he'll be back any day now, when Coy and Jesse get things worked out."

"Well, your mama told me not to come back without you and these kids. She stayed up late last night, baking and cooking. She's planning on y'all staying with her and your sisters till Urbie gets on his feet."

Mama said, "Daddy, I really appreciate Mama sending you, but we need to be here when Urbie gets back."

He knew how strong she felt about keeping her family together and how devastated she still was that he and Granny had separated. The family splintered when her siblings took sides—Mama, Aunt

Helen, and Aunt Bessie siding with him, and Aunt Evelyn, Aunt Madeline, and Uncle Hilas siding with Granny. Mama agreed with Daddy, who said that Granny's judgmental church rules played a big part in Grandpa giving up his engineering job with the Bay Line Railroad, buying his own logging truck, and moving to Charleston to live with Aunt Bessie and Uncle Charlie—he didn't think taking a drink on occasion or not attending church and tithing 10 percent of his hard-earned wages led to eternal damnation. Though Grandpa came home for family occasions, things were never the same, and Mama was determined not to let anything split up *her* family.

I think Mama felt guilty for not confiding in Grandpa about the jugs under the shack. Despite her reservations about Granny's judging Daddy, and not wanting us to be doled out among the relatives, I believe she would have gone with him if the jugs were not there. She told Jip Jones she couldn't take a chance of them being found in Daddy's place. We all felt sad as we waved goodbye and watched swirls of dirt follow Grandpa as he drove away from the shack.

Chapter 3

I am not afraid of storms for I am learning how to sail my ship.

—Louisa May Alcott

After Grandpa left, sheets of rain pelted the shack until dark, leaving a damp, cloudy, and cold black night. As we were getting ready for bed, giggling and being silly, we heard someone walking around our shack. They were making deliberate, heavy footsteps, cracking the thin ice puddles. Mama quietly slipped the shotgun from the rack by the door. With the gun cocked in one hand, she motioned for Robert and Dink to help shove our heavy wooden table against the door. She whispered, "Mack, get the kids to the back of the room and keep them quiet."

Lois, five, was holding one-year-old Bright Eyes in her lap, close to the warmth of the woodstove. She was frozen in her chair, so we stayed with her. The stomping got louder—across the porch and up to the door. We heard a loud knock. Pointing the shotgun in the air, Mama asked, "Who is it?" There was no answer. Again, we heard them stomping around the shack and back onto the porch, then a louder knock. Mama raised her voice, "For the last time, I'm asking who you are and what you want?" No answer. Mama aimed high and pulled the trigger. *Boom!* The blast shook the whole shack and left a huge gaping hole in the wall above the door near the ceiling. We all screamed, and the boots quickly tromped back through the bushes into the woods. Lois, startled by the loud blast, dropped Baby Bright Eyes, who landed on the stove. Dink quickly snatched her up, leaving skin and flesh from wrist to elbow sizzling on the hot surface. Mama was there in a flash to take the wailing baby from Dink. The sickening odor of burning flesh and wool blanket fibers was overwhelming. Cradling the baby, tears streaming down her face, Mama told Dink to mix molasses with baking soda and rip some strips from a clean pillowcase. She plastered the baby's blistered arm with a thick layer of the mixture and bandaged her tiny limb loosely with the strips of cloth. She rocked her gently in her arms, walking the shack in circles. No one said a word. Dink, realizing how cold the shack was getting, told Robert to put more wood in the stove, then climbed upon the table and stuffed a pillow in the massive hole in the wall.

Baby Bright Eyes cried until she was exhausted. When she finally stopped whimpering, Mama sat in the rocker with her bundled in her arms. As she rocked, she whispered to us, "It's going to be okay now, so don't worry. Get some sleep." By then, Robert and Dink had pulled the mattresses from against the wall onto the floor. We all went to bed exhausted, calmed by Mama's humming "Tura-Lura-Lura" and other lullabies and hymns from her youth long into the night.

When Robert went out to get wood the next morning, he flew back into the house, yelling, "Mama, the tires on Daddy's car are slashed. They're as flat as a flitter!" Mama's heart went to her toes. She looked terrified. I guess she knew there was nothing she could do about the tires and that she needed to stay calm. She knew Jip Jones would be coming by in two days. Our prayers were constant—that Baby Evelyn's arm would be all right and that Daddy would show up soon. She checked the baby's arm every few hours and continued plastering the delicate area with the molasses paste.

The next day was centered on Baby Bright Eyes, but Mama tried to distract us. On the third day before Christmas, though we didn't have the ingredients to bake Mama's special Christmas cake and candies, she gathered us in the kitchen area to start our holiday cooking. Mama seemed determined to make everything as traditional as possible. We did our usual housecleaning, and she opened her last jar of applesauce to substitute for eggs to make a cake—not the three-layered lemon-filled cake covered with fluffy coconut frosting that she grew up with, but a sort of applesauce version. She added an extra dab of baking powder and lard so the cake would rise. Normally, we would also make maple and chocolate fudge and divinity with pecans, and chocolate and peanut butter filled taffy, but we settled for molasses pull taffy, without peanut butter. I was happy to help measure the ingredients and pull the taffy. Baby Bright Eyes napped while we made our holiday goodies and sang Christmas carols.

As Jip Jones promised, the morning of Christmas Eve his old truck rumbled up to our porch. Mama was relieved to see him and even more relieved that the redness around the baby's burn had receded considerably.

Jip Jones brought us devastating news from a former local deputy who knew Daddy. The word around the sheriff's office was that Daddy got sentenced to five years. Jip Jones knew Mama was waiting for Daddy to return and get rid of the jugs and would be shaken at the news. It prompted him to make a stop before coming to see us.

He stopped at Sallie's Juke Joint down by the river to talk to Sallie's husband, Joe. He knew Daddy was Joe's best source for shine and that they had declared his to be the best and safest around. Sally, listening to their conversation, blurted, "We will take all the jugs."

Joe added, "It's hard to make safe connections since the new sheriff got elected—and there's a lot of rotgut shine around. We can't trust anybody or anyone's shine nowadays!" Bad moonshine was known to make people go blind—or worse, kill them.

When Jip Jones arrived at our shack, Mama told him about the shotgun incident and the slashed tires. He said, "That's not good, Missus Leila. I can git used tires fo the car, but I don't like all dis bad news I got to tell you." He told her about Joe wanting to buy all the jugs first, then reluctantly, what he heard about Daddy.

At first, she was stunned, biting her lip and shaking her head in disbelief, then she straightened her shoulders and asked, "When can we take the jugs to him?"

"He say he be there tomorrow."

"Good! Tell him, we'll be there tomorrow morning."

He said, "I'll be here in the mornin' to load up mah truck."

Mama said, "Oh no, Jip Jones. I won't have you in prison too! They know your truck around here, but they don't know Urbie's new car yet." She held her hand out to stop him from saying more.

20

Repeating Daddy's words, she said, "Don't worry. With the kids in the car, they won't suspect anything around here."

Jip left and returned that afternoon with four used tires, which he and Robert switched on the car.

Mama got up at daybreak. She quietly woke Dink and Robert and left the rest of us sleeping. They loaded all the jugs from the dirt cellar into Daddy's car and put everything back in place before waking us. She put biscuits in the oven while Mack, Lois, and I got dressed. Then we devoured the delicious, hot, flaky biscuits with generous gobs of Granny's strawberry jam. With tummies full, we rushed to the car during a misty drizzle and crawled in around the jugs. Mama drove away from our shack into the woods, toward Sallie's Juke Joint on the river. Jip Jones would meet us there to negotiate with Joe.

The atmosphere seemed dismal and Mama was quiet, but we were in a good mood as we bounced over the ruts and roots through the forest, and the rain stopped. Mama muttered, "I swear, this is the last time I will ever have anything to do with moonshine!" She would get upset when the subject came up about Daddy being gone. Dink said it was moonshine that caused all the problems—Daddy in prison and Mama's side of the family so mad at Daddy and not liking him. I think they were mad at Mama too, but Mama said her main concern was us kids.

We were bouncing along, and just before the rickety bridge, Robert jumped up and yelled, "Shit!"

Mama reached back and swatted him on the head. "Robert, what in the world…"

She saw why he was alarmed—two men with guns drawn crouched behind a black car blocking the road. Mama took a deep breath, as she slowly came to a stop. I'm sure she was shaking inside but said very calmly, "Don't be afraid, it will be okay," as if to convince herself as well as us. "Keep the kids in the car," she told Dink. As she opened her door and stepped out onto the wet ground, the men lowered their guns and walked toward her.

They recognized Mama. "Well, well, Misses Meeks! Whatta we got here?" A big man with thinning gray hair and his belly hanging over a wide black belt with a shiny badge on it said, "Don't be afraid, kids, but we need you to get out and stand away from the car."

We got out of the car, and Dink took us into the edge of the woods where he pointed. I thought they were going to leave us in the woods, but they just started taking the jugs out of our car and loading them into theirs. The big man looked at Dink and said, "Let me talk to your mama for a minute, and you can get back in the car." He stepped up close to Mama and said in a quiet but stern voice, "Misses Meeks, I'm gonna pretend I didn't catch you with all your young'uns in the car and a load of moonshine. If we catch you hauling again, we'll take your young'uns away from you and send you up to visit their daddy in Atlanta." He turned to the tall, skinny, redheaded man wearing a badge on his dirty T-shirt and said, "Elmer, we got those jugs from that deserted still back in the woods we just left—and not from a car loaded with young'uns, now, didn't we?"

Elmer spat his tobacco on the ground right in front of Mama, as he continued to lean on the front fender of the car. "Yessir, that's just what we done."

The big guy stepped back, looked at Dink, and nodded his head toward our car. We climbed back in as they got into theirs.

Mama's hand was shaking as she turned the key and pressed the starter on the floorboard. The black car backed through some brush into the edge of the woods, allowing us to pass. We pulled away slowly. Mama said nothing. A distance down the winding dirt road, she pulled over and left the engine running. With a slight tremble in her voice, she said, "Thank heavens they were locals from the sheriff's department and *not* the Feds." Dink, sitting beside her, was holding baby Evelyn in a death grip against her chest. Mama reached over, rubbed her shoulder gently, and in a slightly steadier voice, said, "Don't be afraid. Everything's going to be all right now."

Chapter 4

No one is sent to anyone by mistake.
—From *A Course in Miracles*

After the episode with the locals, Mama was quiet. We were too. She seemed to be in deep thought as she navigated the twisting trail back to the shack. Her eyes were glued to the dirt road, as if answers to her dilemma would appear in the dust engulfing us. She parked close to the front door and, before turning off the engine, turned to Dink and said, "Let's get packed. We're going back home to Millville." This brought resounding cheers from the back seat.

She added, "If we hop to it, we can be there before dark."

Mama often said, "We're only 125 miles from home, but it feels like a thousand." I was tired of Daddy's adventure too—I wanted to go back to the home we'd left in the middle of the night, the home I was having a hard time remembering. I wanted to play with Aunt Evelyn's fluffy white Persian cat that Lois was always talking about and try to catch one of Granny's chickens.

As we were getting out of the car, Robert asked Mama, "Can we go to Granny's?"

She quickly answered, "No, we're going to our own home, and none of you are going to be doled out to your aunts. That is not up for question, so don't get any ideas if they start discussing that, because we're all staying together! Is that understood?"

We answered, "Yes, ma'am."

Baby Bright Eyes napped while Lois and I played nearby. Gathering things to be loaded, Mama said, "We'll use our quilts for pallets to sleep on and borrow some of Granny's to keep warm, until

23

I can figure out how to get the mattresses and stove to our house." She stood in the middle of the shack with her hand on her forehead as she looked from the stove to the mattresses and muttered, "I just hope they'll still be here."

They stuffed everything possible in the car: the few groceries, including the dry contents of the cans in pillowcases and lard in a pot, the kerosene stove and lamps, quilts and blankets, Baby Bright Eyes's molasses mixture, diapers, clothes, and Mama's shotgun. She told Mack and Robert to take the decorations off the tree and find a place for them in the car. They filled every nook and cranny, hardly leaving room for Mama to drive and us to sit on each other's laps. Mama ran her hand over the side rail of Baby Bright Eyes's crib and gave the arm of her rocker a gentle push before she closed the door.

We were arguing by the car, negotiating who would sit where, when Grandpa's logging truck rumbled up. Granny apparently had commissioned him again to get Mama and us out of the woods. We forgot our negotiations and ran to meet him. As he stepped down, he looked relieved. He said, "Well, Leila, I'm mighty glad I don't have to tie you up, like your mama suggested, to get you and the kids out of here."

In a choked voice, she said, "It's good to see you, Daddy. I don't need convincing, but I could sure use a big hug and some prayers." As she hugged him, she added, "I guess you…know…"

He put both hands on her shoulders, tilted his head back, and looked in her eyes. "Leila, everything is going to be alright. Let's get the rest of your things loaded and get you all to your Mama's house."

She pulled back, wiping her eyes with the back of her hand. "Daddy, I'm not going to pile in on Mama, and I'm not doling the kids out to anyone." She knew Granny thought of Daddy as the worst kind of sinner and that she was, too, for "wallowing with the swine," as she heard her mama once say of someone else. She had been unable to make Granny understand. She added, "Daddy, I just want to get the kids back in school and in their own home. I will sell Urbie's car and get some laundry jobs, and we will manage just fine."

"Now, Leila, you know your mama's going to insist you stay with her till you get on your feet. Consider staying at least till I get Urbie's car sold."

Grandpa, Mama, and Robert loaded things in the truck we could not have taken in the car—Baby Bright Eyes's bed and rocker, mattresses, storage cans, and Mama's treasured cedar chest that Grandpa made for her right after her first infant died from a fever. As Grandpa was securing everything, he said, "Leila, I'll have to come back with help to load that cast-iron stove." The boys climbed into the cab with Grandpa. Lois and I jumped into the back of the car, and Dink got in the front with Baby Bright Eyes.

Mama hesitated, then stepped on the running board and yelled, "Daddy, we'll do it! We'll go to Mama's."

He smiled and stuck his hand out the window with a thumbs-up.

We followed the trail of dust behind Grandpa's truck as we left the forest and turned north on the paved road toward Granny's.

I believe Mama was quiet because she was reminiscing. Lois and I played our usual guessing games, counted cars, and giggled in the back seat, while Dink entertained the baby playing "This little piggy..."

After a while Dink became quiet as she watched Mama drive. Finally, she spoke up and reluctantly asked, "Mama, I've always wondered...would this be a good...can I ask...how can George, Luvera, Ithaniel, Verna, and Nellie be our sisters and brothers if you're not their real mama?" She was referring to our older siblings who came along before Dink, Robert, Mack, Lois, and me.

Mama glanced up from the road and, biting her lip as she often did when she was working something out, said, "I guess having siblings that are almost my age *is* confusing. You're old enough to know, and this is as good a time as any. I'll try to explain why you have older siblings...

"I believe you know that Verna and Nellie's mama was my first cousin Annie who grew up next door to me and my family. Her mama and Granny were sisters. She was almost eight years older than me, but she was my favorite cousin and my hero. I believe she was Granny's favorite as well. She was kind, funny, and always had a smile for everyone. Verna and Nellie got their beauty from Annie, and Nellie got her sweet disposition from her, but I don't know where Verna got that temper.

"When she was eighteen, Annie received a letter with a proposal of marriage from your daddy, after his wife and baby died during child birth. He needed a mama for his three motherless children: George, Luvera, and Ithaniel. She only knew him slightly, but your grandpa—my daddy and Annie's favorite uncle—knew him well. Before Grandpa moved to Charleston after he and Granny divorced, he was an engineer on the Bay Line Railroad. He engineered the train that hauled the logs from the forests where your daddy ran logging crews. He told Annie your daddy was a good, hardworking, honest man—so, typical for the times in 1918 when girls who were not married by age eighteen were considered 'old maids,' Annie accepted his proposal and became a mama to George, Luvera, and Ithaniel.

"But soon all the forests around North Florida were logged out. Mr. Sherman, who owned the old sawmill, opened a new one in the Glades, where there were thousands of acres of forests, so they moved to Okeechobee in the Glades of South Florida.

"By the time they were married eight years, Annie had Verna and Nellie, and she was expecting twins. She had complications with her pregnancy, and her doctor ordered her to stay in bed until the babies were born. George was in the Navy, and Luvera was married, living in Tallahassee, so since I was out of school for the summer, Granny sent me to help her."

We were listening intently, and I could just picture the scene: Mama stepping off the train in Okeechobee, shading her eyes against the blaring Everglades sun. The knot tightened in her stomach as she looked around for her cousin's husband. She had not seen him since he and Annie were married eight years before. She was afraid she wouldn't recognize him, but Daddy recognized Mama in her home-made long-sleeved dress, clutching a battered suitcase in a death grip. She stared at two young ladies on the platform with bobbed hair smoking cigarettes, wearing red lipstick, short dresses, and long beads. The pretty blond said, "Be careful there, honey," as Mama tripped when she walked past them.

When Mama arrived that summer day in 1925, the Glades was notorious for being a mobster hideout. Moonshiners, gamblers, and outlaws lived there—including the infamous John Ashley, whose gang robbed banks and trains—but only took the money belonging to the wealthy—and had shoot-outs with lawmen.

The Roaring Twenties was in full swing; the Glades area was known as the Chicago of the South. Mama had no idea she would not be returning to her home to finish her sophomore year at Millville High.

*****

"Your daddy picked me up from the train and took me to their little house, surrounded with papaya and fig trees, with a chicken coop and a garden in the back. When we arrived, Annie, still in her nightgown, was kneeling in the garden with the children, attempting to gather vegetables. She looked weak but approached me with open arms and a welcome smile. As we embraced, I realized she had a slight fever—or she could have just been warm from the beastly summer heat of the Everglades. I said, 'Annie, I believe you're running a fever. Aren't you supposed to be in bed?'

"She said, 'The kids wanted to go outside, and they love to pick vegetables.'

"We got her settled, and she promised she would follow doctor's orders, now that I was there, so your daddy returned to work. Though she seemed to sleep a lot and sometimes ran a low-grade fever, her doctor just told her to take aspirin and stay off her feet.

"I kept a pot of chicken soup on the stove—about the only thing she would eat—kept the kids quiet when she slept, and tried to cool her skin with damp cloths. As the days passed, I grew attached to the kids, and Annie and I became close as we laughed at them—about how Verna bossed her older brother and little sister around and they followed her orders. We reminisced and exchanged family stories.

"I had been there almost a month, when I had one of the worst days of my life. When I brought her breakfast, she was burning up with fever, and my knees almost buckled at the sight of blood on the sheets. She had started hemorrhaging. I didn't want to look alarmed and cause Annie or the kids to panic. I didn't know what to do. I prayed for God's help, and with the calmest yet most authoritative voice I could muster, I told Ithaniel, who was eight, to be a big boy and run as fast as he possibly could to the mill, almost a mile down the road, to get his daddy.

"I continued to pray as I wiped her forehead and wrists with cool, wet cloths and whispered, 'Everything will be all right, Annie. Urbie will be right here to take you to the doctor.'

"Her breathing was shallow and her voice hardly audible. 'Don't worry, Leila…doctor…will know…'

"I thought of Granny and Annie's mama and the many prayer chains they started when someone was in trouble or sick, and I wished I could tell them to ask everyone to pray.

"Waiting for your daddy felt like an eternity, but before long we heard the car door slam. He had Annie in the car in a flash and on the way to the doctor, who told him to get her to the hospital. He rushed her by train to the closest hospital, sixty-four miles away, in West Palm Beach, where they performed an emergency caesarean. I was horrified to learn her babies were stillborn. She remained in the hospital a week, and then my heart was broken when she died of complications from the surgery. I was so distraught I didn't know what to think or do.

"Ithaniel seemed to know something tragic had happened, but I didn't know how to answer Little Nellie and Verna when they asked, 'When will Mama come home?'

"Annie and the twins were buried in the Meeks' family plot beside the Baptist church, near the farm where your daddy grew up. After the funeral, George returned to the Navy and Luvera and her family to Tallahassee. I returned home. School would soon start, and back then, a woman would never stay in a house with a man without his wife, unless in this case, I became his wife." She looked over at

Dink, who was listening but looked a little confused. "It's complicated, Dink." She paused before continuing.

"Within weeks, however, your daddy asked me to return to Okeechobee to become his wife and a mama to Ithaniel, Verna, and Nellie. I was as surprised as Granny, who was vehemently opposed to me getting married, especially to someone much older than me, but Grandpa said, 'Minnie, sometimes, age is only a number. Leila's almost sixteen, and she could do a lot worse around here than Urbie, who's a good man and the hardest worker I have ever come across. He'll be a good provider.'

"I surely didn't want to hurt Granny, and though I struggled with the right thing to do, I just felt in my heart that I should return to Okeechobee and marry your daddy to help with Ithaniel, Verna, and Nellie. At first, I was concerned about the kids needing me and never thought about the age difference. He was a real good daddy, and he had a wonderful way about him—he always found good in people and made the hardest challenges seem like fun—so it wasn't hard to fall in love with him.

"So, you see…though you have different mamas, you really are sisters and brothers because you all have the same daddy. This was common back then, when more young women died from childbirth than any other cause.

"Another thing that was common back then, children did what their parents expected of them, but I defied Granny. I'm happy that I married your daddy and helped with your older siblings until they grew up with families of their own, and I'm very glad that I have all of you—but I am sad that fifteen years have passed and Granny is still upset."

Mama's story entranced us, especially learning how Mama and Daddy met and about our other sisters and brothers. Time passed quickly, and we soon pulled up to Granny's house. Wonderful whiffs of Granny's cooking met us as she met us on the porch, wiping her hands on her apron. Her hair was braided and twisted in a heap on top of her head, adding a few inches to her tiny frame. We all got big, long hugs. When it was my turn came, I noted with satisfaction that familiar smell of Granny's talcum powder. Mama seemed hesitant, but she stepped forward and gave Granny a hug.

Inside, I was struck speechless to see a tall Christmas tree with an angel touching the ceiling of the little room. The tree sparkled with silver garland and tinsel, colored balls hanging from every branch, and small red candles burning in little holders on the branch tips. Gifts were stacked under the tree. We would have a Christmas after all. This would remain one of the brightest memories of my childhood. The table was spread with two stuffed roasted chickens, sweet potatoes, butterbeans, corn, a pumpkin pie, and the famous coconut cake with fluffy icing.

Mama knew Granny had spent all her savings from her firewood money. Her hard feelings about Granny disapproving of her and Daddy melted into gratitude. "Thank you, Mama," she said in a choked voice. "This is really special for the kids…and me."

Chapter 5

Adversity has the effect of eliciting talents which, in prosperous circumstances, would have lain dormant.
　　—Horace (Quintus Horatius Flaccus), *Satires*

Mama registered Dink, Robert, and Mack in school, and ironically, Dink got Bessie Gainer for her teacher—the same teacher Mama had not many years before—who was quick to use a ruler with little regard for where the whack connected. When Mama was in her class, the ruler was the subject of a discussion between Ms. Gainer and Granny. That's when she learned of Granny's Irish temper. Granny told Dink, "If she ever hits you with that ruler, you come home and let me know." She did just that! The windows of Bessie Gainer's classroom came almost to the floor and were always open. Ms. Gainer was marching up and down the aisles, picking up homework. Dink had left hers at home. When she told Dink to hold out her hand for a whack, Dink sprang from her desk, jumped out the open window, and ran home to Granny's. When Granny revisited Ms. Gainer to discuss the ruler again, Mama was reminded that though Granny could be outspoken and quick to judge, she was passionate about protecting those she loved. Mama smiled, knowing Granny and Dink had this under control.

Mama kept Baby Bright Eyes, Lois, and me out from underfoot, but she let us help pick beans from the garden to be canned and watch as she and Granny poured a mixture of lye, borax, and ammonia into a big pot of grease that cooled over a fire in the backyard to make the year's supply of lye soap. While at Granny's, we did the thing Mama said she dreaded the most—we attended church

31

Monday and Wednesday nights and Sundays. Mama sang as Granny played the piano. We were careful not to dance or to sing the wrong songs around Granny. We were there only two weeks when Grandpa sold Daddy's car. Aunt Evelyn secured a job for Mama to do washing and ironing for the owner of the furniture store where she was a decorator, and we moved back into our own house. Granny tried to insist Mama allow at least one or two of us stay with our aunts, but Mama stood her ground.

We got our first letter from Daddy a few days later. He sounded like his old self, asking about Mama and us kids and saying he was optimistic that he'd soon be home. "There are books here to learn just about anything you want to know," he wrote.

Typical for the early 1900s, he'd dropped out of school after third grade to help on the farm; however, he had a curious mind and a passion for reading *The Farmers' Almanac*, so books would excite him. He loved nature and the farm. At an early age, he worked on tools and farm equipment to make them more efficient, but watching his parents work from sunup to sundown, struggling just to exist, prompted him to want to be more than a farmer. He left the farm in his midteens to work in logging and find a better way of life.

In his letters, he always had funny things to tell us and included positive quotes that he found in books, such as the one from Franklin D. Roosevelt: "When you reach the end of your rope, tie a knot and hang on." Mama would write to him about what good students the kids were, that we missed him, and that we were doing fine.

Uncle Jesse and Coy Rushing continued to do their best to get Daddy released, and Mama endured, hoping they would succeed. We planted a garden and bought some chickens. Mama's sisters occasionally came to bring things they said they had too much of, and neighbors who had gotten groceries on credit from our store—before we had to close the store—would sometimes drop by with a casserole or whatever they could spare, but Mama still had to pinch pennies. About the time Mama needed to "tie that knot in the rope," an owner of a Chinese laundry whom Uncle Jesse knew offered to drop laundry off for her to iron.

Each morning she rose early to make breakfast. On washdays she would rise early, make breakfast, prime the pump out back, and start filling wash tubs. When Dink and Robert finished breakfast, they would help her fill four tubs before going to school—one for boiling laundry, one for scrubbing, and two for rinsing. She did inside chores while the morning chill eased before starting to scrub and spent most of her waking hours over a washtub or an ironing board, while humming or singing without a complaint.

Though we'd see our aunts pretty regularly, we only saw Granny when we walked to her house with Robert when he went to chop wood. Mama told Aunt Helen that Granny was upset because we stopped going to church after we moved back home. Mama said, "Everyone is really nice to my face, Helen, but I hear what they say: 'Poor Leila with that sinner for a husband in prison,' and I don't want the kids to hear such things."

Aunt Helen said, "I know, Leila. We've heard how 'everything is a sin and everybody a sinner' all our lives. What happened to 'Judge not, and you will not be judged'?"

Mama said, "I wish I didn't get so angry with Mama. I guess I do my share of judging too."

Aunt Helen said, "I guess we all do."

Mama said, "I know God understands what's going on, and I'll rely on him to do all the judging."

Months passed, with more letters to and from Daddy with more quotes: "Books are for people who wish they were somewhere else" (Mark Twain). He also told us he was reading about how John and Lillian Gilbreth, known as foremost efficiency experts for time and motion study, revolutionized the engineering of construction jobs, improving efficiency on construction sites, in workplaces, and in homes. He told Mama to try ways to save time and energy, such as moving her wash station close to the pump. This got Mama thinking, and she made an apron to have clothespins at hand rather than chasing a bag hanging on the clothesline. She rearranged dishes, pots, pans, and groceries to a more workable location and put the baby's diapers next to the crib. In another letter, he told us, "I'm working on plans to build a perpetual motion machine. This machine will create energy to run itself without a battery or electricity and will make us a whole lot of money." We started referring to Daddy's invention as *Daddy's magic machine.*

*****

Our aunts always wanted us to sing, and Aunt Evelyn liked to say, "I have a dime for the first one who sings a song for me." She especially liked the silly ones she had never heard as a child. I was too shy to sing except with others after supper or in church, but Lois would always jump up and say, "I'll sing." When she sang "The Happy Little Woodpecker Song," "He's up this morning bright and ear-ly—to wake up all the neigh-bor-hood…," Aunt Evelyn told her, "I have a friend at the radio station who would want you to sing that on his *Good Morning Show.* If I buy you a new dress and shoes to wear, will you sing this song for him?"

She immediately said, "Yes, I'll sing it."

Mama finally agreed after we begged her to let us hear Lois sing on the radio, but she told Aunt Evelyn, "I know she'll sing for you, but I'm sure she won't sing for a stranger, because she won't even sing in Sunday school by herself." Aunt Evelyn asked Mama if Lois could stay with her a few days to practice. Mama reluctantly agreed.

Several days later, when Aunt Evelyn took her to the station, Lois didn't want to get out of the car, and when she did, she stood in front of the microphone and refused to open her mouth. She told Aunt Evelyn she would after she practiced more. They came by the house to see if Mama would allow her to stay a couple more days with Aunt Evelyn and try again. Lois flitted around in her new pink dress, shiny shoes, and blond curls in pink ribbons. When we tried to hug her, she would push us away, saying, "You'll mess up my hair and dress."

Looking at her with narrowed eyes, Mama said, "Lois, go get your play clothes on, because you're not going anywhere." Years later, Lois and I laughed about how she got her new dress and shoes taken away and flitted right back into the family fold.

Mama was hanging clothes when Uncle Jesse drove up. Untying the bag of clothespins from her waist, she dropped them into the basket and hurried toward him. He waved and yelled, "Leila, I've got some good news!" Mama stopped in her tracks and held her breath, as he approached. "Coy called this morning to tell us Urbie's sentence has been reduced to one year."

"He's been gone ten months already…does that mean…he'll be home Christmas?"

"Possibly. Coy said it's a done deal."

Tears tumbled from her eyes down her chin, onto her clasped hands, as she looked up to say a prayer of thanks. She hugged Uncle Jesse and said, "This is the best news I've had all year, thank you! I was beginning to wonder if God had forsaken us."

He gave her a slight squeeze and said, "I do hope he's home for Christmas."

Mama told Lois and me, "As soon as I finish hanging the clothes, we're going to bake our special cake before the kids get home from school." Mama grew up associating Granny's coconut cake with lemon filling and fluffy white icing covered with coconut for special occasions. This cake became a family tradition for special occasions.

When Lois asked what the surprise was, Mama replied, "I want you to all be together when I tell you. When Dink, Robert, and Mack come home from school, we'll have the cake on the table and you, Buzz, and I will yell 'Surprise,' then I'll tell all of you at once. Is that okay?" We thought that would be fun. We loved surprises.

We had the cake baked and on the table. Just before time for them to get home, Mama told Lois to stand outside the door and tell them to all come in together for a surprise. I couldn't wait! We whooped and hollered and hugged Mama when she told us the good news. We ate cake to celebrate, then had more after supper. Mama hardly ate, but she looked happier than I had seen her in a long time. We played our instruments, sang, and danced beyond bedtime.

Our spindly Christmas tree had no lights, but Mama hung strings of dried berries, her faded balls, and many homemade decorations. She baked another special cake and cooked for two days before Christmas, but the second fluffy white coconut cake and our traditional candies would remain safely inside the kitchen cabinet until Daddy returned. We posted messages welcoming him home on torn pieces of paper on the porch and throughout the house, then waited anxiously for him to come. We put cookies and milk out for Santa, but the special cake for Daddy was still untouched.

On Christmas Day, the silence of dawn was broken by the crowing of our rooster, Chipper, from his perch on the top of the henhouse. Mama was changing Baby Evelyn's diaper, Dink was piling more wood on the dying embers, and the rest of us were beginning to stir. Mama was the first to hear Uncle Jesse's car stop out front. She said, "Kids, get up! Get up! I think your Daddy's coming!" Handing the baby to Dink, she flew through the front door in her bare feet and flannel nightgown. Dink shut the door against the cold, grabbed a blanket from the bed, and rebundled Baby Bright Eyes. We all jumped up and flocked to the window, then tripped over each other getting through the door. Daddy jumped out the passenger side of the car before Uncle Jesse turned off the engine. We almost knocked him down, piling on top, hugging, laughing, and crying at the same time.

"My god, I missed my young'uns and you, Shorty!"

Tears streamed down her cheeks as she looked up at him. As we clung to him, he gripped Robert's and Mack's shoulders and said, "Sons, let me tell you something. Prison is no place you ever want to be!" Reaching his arm around Mama's waist, he squeezed her and kissed her on the cheek. She gripped his hand and lifted it to her lips.

Mama said, "Let's get inside by the fire, before we freeze to death out here." Uncle Jesse took two paper sacks from the back seat, holding Daddy's few belongings, and handed them to Robert. Once inside, Daddy rummaged through them and pulled out a foot-long red-and-white striped peppermint stick candy and an orange for each of us. And from that day and long after we were grown, peppermint sticks always hung from the branches of our Christmas trees. We never stopped feeling that joy.

Since Daddy returned and was now an ex-con, no one wanted to hire him. Daddy said, "Millville is a dry county, because they voted to keep the sinners out. But there's no shortage of moonshine or judgmental preachers and churchgoers who consume the shine."

So Mama spent weeks over a washtub or ironing board, while he searched relentlessly for work. Nights, he worked on plans for his magic machine. Hovering over big sheets of drawings spread on the table with a single lightbulb dangling overhead, he worked into the wee hours, more determined than ever to invent his machine. He just needed a job so he could afford to build it. Then our fortune would be made.

His search for work extended beyond the Florida border before he finally landed a job in Alabama, several hours north of Millville, supplying a field crew and managing them to harvest peanuts for a big farm; but he didn't have a vehicle, let alone a truck or a crew. But he did some labor on Uncle Jesse's house and got a small loan from Grandpa and bought an old truck. He enclosed the back with benches and hired twelve men including Jip Jones, and just like that, he was back in business.

The farm needed an additional crew for another crop. Even though Uncle Fletcher was an evangelical preacher in Panama City who had somewhat disassociated himself from Daddy. Daddy told the farmer he had a brother with a crew and called him. Daddy always looked after his four younger brothers and sister since Uncle Ed died, leaving him to be the oldest.

I never knew anyone Mama didn't like, except Uncle Fletcher. She said he never appreciated the many things Daddy did for him; he was mean to his wife and kids and didn't adhere to what he preached. Daddy teased, "If I get him this job, maybe he will offer some indulgences for my sinful soul."

Uncle Fletcher showed up with a truck and crew and went to work.

Daddy always had a way of making work seem like fun. He worked along with his crew, challenging them to work faster by creating rewards for the fastest and joke prizes for the slowest. He often gave them endearing nicknames, and they usually liked having Daddy's personal acknowledgment—but not always. When Jip Jones first came to work with us, Daddy nicknamed him Ace. Daddy said he was an "ace" among the cotton pickers, but Jip Jones said, "Mista Urbie, sir, mah name ain't Ace. Mah name is Jip Jones."

So Daddy said, "Okay. Jip Jones, it is," and it stuck. Like my name, I wished I could have told him my name wasn't Buzz, that my name was Betty Sue, but I guess I waited too long. Because he named me that as a baby, my brothers loved calling me Buzzzzz, and my nickname stuck.

Daddy was always joking and jousting with his crew. This soon created a problem between him and his brother, who always wore white shirts and used a different style of management. He warned Daddy, "Urb, you're the boss, and you need to make them know that." Before long, Uncle Fletcher's men didn't want to work for him—they wanted to join Daddy's crew. Even though Daddy wouldn't hire them, Uncle Fletcher accused him of trying to steal his men, and it caused a fracture in their relationship that took some time to mend.

After a few paychecks, Daddy started building a huge structure in our backyard, which cost a lot of his pay and all his spare time. Daddy's magic machine looked like a Ferris wheel. When the season ended, he put his project on hold until he could find more work. When time passed and he found none, he called Uncle Vester, who suggested we return to the Glades where Daddy knew people who would help. He offered to have us stay with him and the Taylors, who lived with him. They were close friends of Mama's and Daddy's from way back. I believe they met during a crisis when the Depression forced them and other families to move into shanties, forming a Hooverville, where they joined forces to survive.

Daddy hated to leave his unfinished machine, and Mama was sad to leave our house, but they knew he had a better chance of survival in the Glades. The Glades was a different world. Locals looked at moonshining to feed your family and help your neighbors. Businessmen and politicians looked at them as essential during Prohibition to supply hotels and restaurants in South Florida for tourism. The local lawmen looked at them for additional income from payoffs, so they warded off the Feds from interfering in their territory. Daddy was well-known and respected in the Glades. He didn't know what he would do, but he promised Mama, "It won't involve moonshine."

Hooverville shanty, Canal Point, Fl.
(photo by Marion Post Wolcott)

Chapter 6

What lies behind us and what lies before us are tiny matters compared to what lies within us.
—Henry Stanley Haskins

We left Millville early Friday morning. We finally arrived at our destination late Sunday afternoon—a little dot on the map on the northwest side of Belle Glade called Chosen. We saw a sign with an arrow, "Slim's Fish Camp 1 mile ahead," and turned left onto a dirt road that ended at a gravel driveway in front of a white house with dark-green trim. Uncle Vester, Uncle Jim, and Aunt Rhodie were sitting in rocking chairs, drinking sweet tea. Uncle Vester stood and raised his glass as we approached, then hurried down the steps to where we parked. Uncle Jim, who had a deformed back, stumbled up from his chair and clung to the porch rail as he and Aunt Rhodie stood by the top step and waved. Their kids, Marilee, Lili Mae, and Louise, playing on a tire swing hanging from a big tree beside the house, smiled and waved. We were exhausted but relieved and happy to receive such a warm welcome.

The Taylors lived in the shanties on the ridge in Canal Point when Mama, Daddy, and others banded together to survive the Depression, just as many immigrants do today. I think Uncle Vester got spooked and bought the store to have a legal means of income after Daddy got caught and went to prison when he followed Mama. Uncle Vester was not one to stay put inside to run a store, so I believe he wanted the Taylors to live with him so he'd have a good cook and someone to run his store. I never knew what was wrong with Uncle Jim's back, but I don't believe he could do physical work.

As Daddy got out of the truck, he said, "Oh my god, I smell Rhodie's biscuits! Let me out of here." Everyone laughed. Daddy gave his younger brother a hardy handshake and slung his arm across his shoulders as they went up the steps, where he shook hands with Uncle Jim and hugged Aunt Rhodie. The ladies embraced and chatted as if nine years had not passed since they'd hauled water from the lake to cook and do laundry, planted gardens, canned, and skinned catfish and alligators to survive. She asked Mama about our older sisters and brothers, and Mama caught her up to date on their marriages and families. As they chatted nonstop, they went inside then reappeared with glasses of ice and a pitcher of sweet tea.

I sipped my tea and stood back clutching the glass, not knowing quite how to approach our new friends, who, we were told, were like family. Dink, Robert, and Mack were the same age as their kids. Mack and Louise were too young to remember anyone, but in a short time, we felt like we'd known each other all our lives. We played outside on the tire swing and a couple of games of kick-the-can and red rover, until Aunt Rhodie called us to wash up at the pump for supper. The smell of fried chicken interfered with concentrating on our game anyway; we had been eating peanut butter and apple butter sandwiches for the last three days. Aunt Rhodie must have cooked all day. We feasted on turnips, fried chicken, baked sweet potatoes, fresh green beans, swamp cabbage slaw, and two big pans of biscuits. After a long day, with tummies stuffed, there were no complaints when quilts were spread on every inch of open floor in the kitchen and living room, and we were told to claim a pallet for the night. We were so tired there was soon only sounds of Mama and Aunt Rhodie's muffled voices from the porch over the eerie sounds of crickets.

We had been there a week, and though Mama knew Aunt Rhodie loved us being there, she didn't like crowding them. On his way home from the store, Uncle Jim brought two baskets of beans and one of tomatoes from the packing house for them to can. Mama was glad to have some way to help, like the times they worked together on the ridge. They rose early the next morning to start canning, talking, and laughing as they filled mason jars.

"How in the world did you manage with six kids while Urbie was in prison, Leila?" Aunt Rhodie asked as she pulled the second basket of beans between them.

Mama answered, "By the grace of God, Rhodie."

"I want to hear everything that's happened since I saw you last, Leila—everything!"

Mama reminded Aunt Rhodie that she'd been expecting almost any day when she and the kids left Canal Point after Granny sent Grandpa to bring Dink, Robert, and Mack to live with them that December in 1933. "Though we had moved from the shanties, into houses on the ridge, the Feds knew Urbie and Vester were still making moonshine. Well, Lois was born weeks after we arrived at Mama's. Cindy, the same midwife who delivered me twenty-eight years earlier, delivered her. Urbie soon followed me to Millville and bought a piece of property a mile down the road from Mama and Daddy's. He built a grocery store with living quarters attached in the back to reclaim his family and show Mama he could provide for us legally. He stocked the shelves and opened the store, and we moved in before completion. I was thankful to have our family back together in our own home. I made curtains from fabric Mama gave me and braided rugs out of rags. The kids and I planted a big garden at the first breath of spring. All was going well. Buzz was born right after Christmas two years later. The Depression was still stifling the nation. Some people were still hanging on, and others had lost hope. You know Urbie—he allowed credit for those who couldn't make ends meet, and the shelves of our store were soon bare, with no money to restock. He had been looking for work, but jobs were few and far between. He finally found a steady job that required him to stay out of town occasionally. Things were much better. I had groceries to cook, which was a big relief, since I was expecting again. I was thankful we were away from the free rein of moonshine and hiding out—actually, I was glad Bay County voted to remain dry, and moonshine was less tolerated.

"One night when Buzz was two and Urbie was working out of town, we were awakened by screeching tires and brakes, then the loud slam of the door of his old truck near the entrance to the back door. He blasted through the kitchen door, yelling, 'Leila, wake up, quick! Get the kids in the truck fast. We gotta get out of here.' I was into my seventh month and not feeling well, but I moved fast without asking questions. I grabbed the quilts from our beds, rushed back into the house to help gather essentials, and Urbie was shouting at Dink and Robert to help me load the truck while he got the tent and camping gear. The truck had high slatted wooden sides with a canvas top. In a matter of minutes, the older kids were climbing into the back around our two-burner kerosene stove, pots and pans, cans of dried beans, rice, and other staples, including army blankets and quilts. I grabbed Buzz and jumped in the cab, and as Urbie opened his door to slide under the wheel, he yelled to the kids in the back, 'We're going on a fun adventure!' I didn't want to believe it and didn't say anything, but I knew he just had to be involved with moonshine again. I was sick at heart when it hit me that he didn't know the new sheriff of Bay County and didn't have the political friends he had in the Glades."

*****

Mama told Aunt Rhodie all about Daddy's Adventure—how we watched swirling clouds of dust from the back of the truck as we sped down the highway and across the Florida state line, how they switched off driving and we kept moving, only stopping for gas and letting the engine cool enough to pour water into the overheated radiator. Mama made peanut butter and grape jelly sandwiches to eat on the road, while Daddy checked the tires and kept the truck running. We didn't stop until we saw the aqua-blue waters of the Gulf bordering the road through Biloxi, Mississippi. We drove through the night and the next day. The sky was dark and filled with stars before Daddy steered onto a dirt road into a wooded area and turned off the engine. He draped the tent from one side of the back of the truck and spread army blankets underneath on the ground, where he and our brothers slept for the night. Mama, Dink, Lois, and I slept in the back of the truck.

The next morning, we got up early and hardly stopped until we reached Texarkana, Texas, where Daddy looked for work, without luck. We stopped at numerous farmhouses where he asked everyone we encountered about work. He finally talked to a farmer who, seeing us kids, Daddy's desperation, and Mama's condition, hired him to help build a pigpen. He told Daddy we could set up camp by his barn while we looked for other work. Two days later, another farmer hired him for the day to haul bales of hay from the fields and stack them in his barn, but no one could afford to pay a living wage. Daddy talked to a burly Mexican man who was fueling his beat-up old truck: "Howdy do, sir? I'm Urbie Meeks. My family and I are looking for work, and I'm wondering where you might be working?"

The gentleman said in a broken accent, as he shook his head from side to side and reached out with upturned palms, "No work... no work." Daddy thanked him as he patted his shoulder and turned and scuffed back to the truck where we were all waiting. He looked desperate. Mama was scared, but Daddy cracked jokes to keep her spirits up.

When Mama said, "Urbie, maybe we should get a little closer to home," he did a U-turn and headed east.

We followed the back roads as much as possible but stopped in Biloxi, where Mama persuaded Daddy to let us play in the water to cool off. He parked on a side road lined with fish houses and unpainted, weathered shotgun homes with little front porches. There were abandoned wooden boats and rusty automobiles, half hidden by high weeds, in surrounding yards. We played in the water while Daddy talked to the men around the fish houses. Most of them were looking for work too. When we returned to the truck, Daddy was cleaning fish the fishermen had given him. He built a fire beside the truck, and Mama cooked a delicious meal of fresh fish and grits before we drove farther east through Mossy Point, Mississippi, and into Alabama.

On a back road in Grand Bay, Alabama, we came upon a big field of white cotton, ready to be picked, but there was no one picking. Daddy said, "Maybe they're just getting their crew together, and we can join them." We followed the dirt road beside the long field of white and passed an abandoned, dilapidated little house surrounded with high weeds and a collapsed barn behind it. We continued until we came upon a bigger, unpainted house with a front porch surrounded with pink-and-blue hydrangea and a swing on the far end. Daddy parked by the porch, near the door, and walked up the wide steps. As he approached the screen door, a white-haired gentleman wearing a worn long-john shirt and baggy pants held up with wide black suspenders leaned on his cane as he opened the door. Daddy took off his hat and said, "Howdy do, sir. I'm Urbie Meeks, and I'm looking for work." He pointed down the road. "Would you happen to know who the crew boss is for that field of cotton back there? We're in mighty bad need of work and a place to set up our tent." We were all watching from the truck window or peeping around the side of the back. The old gentleman stepped out and closed the door behind him. They talked for a few minutes, and Daddy returned to the truck with a spring in his step.

"Boy, are we in luck, Shorty. That's Mr. Stokes, and he owns that field of cotton. Early summer made his crop come in early, and his crew hasn't finished down in Florida yet. He needs the crop picked now."

Mama said, "But, Urbie, we can't pick that whole field of cotton."

"Well, here's the best part. We made a deal. I'll go to Biloxi and pick up a crew. He'll pay for what we pick and a percentage of the returns of all the cotton when I take it to the gin. Mr. Stokes said I was an answer to his prayers, but I'll tell you—he had it all backwards."

Mama said, "Oh, thank heavens! I just knew something would work out."

Daddy added, "He said the crew could camp out in that old barn, and we were welcomed to stay in that little run-down house in front, if it makes a better shelter than our tent." That was good news for Mama. She'd take a solid floor in a dilapidated house any day over a floor of dirt.

They drove back down the dirt road and through the high weeds to the front of the old house. Daddy cleared a path to the door with his machete, and they unloaded our meager belongings. Daddy and Robert dragged loose boards from a collapsed shed behind the house to reinforce a couple of shelves and counters in the kitchen area. Mama and Dink set up the kerosene stove to make supper. While Mama was cooking, Dink got the kids settled and Daddy and Robert built benches inside the back of the truck on both sides and behind the cab to transport a crew from Biloxi.

After we had hoecakes with jelly for breakfast the next morning, Daddy and Robert left early. Biloxi was only forty-two miles away, but Daddy told Mama they would be gone most of the day. He wanted to take plenty of time to talk to each of his potential workers long enough to learn their character—and if they could pick cotton. They got home late afternoon. Daddy rumbled the truck across the weeds to the front of the barn. There were eight men and two of their wives scrunched onto the benches, and three children on the floor between them. The two boys looked as if they were Robert's age, and the little girl, Lois's age. Daddy and Robert helped them unload their things. Daddy came back up to our place and said we should go down and meet everyone. Mama and the women seemed to be glad to have females to relate to. We kids all got along immediately. Daddy especially liked Jip Jones. He told Mama, "You can tell that one's gonna be a good worker. You look at his hands and know he's not afraid of hard work."

Daddy spent the next morning working out all the details with Mr. Stokes. They seemed to like each other. Mr. Stokes appreciated Daddy's knowledge of farming and running crews. He gave Daddy the long sacks that would be slung over the pickers' shoulders and the keys to his work truck to haul the cotton to the gin. Daddy said to Mama, "Since I'm the only one in our family who's ever picked cotton, I sure hope we have a good crew." Dink, Robert, and Mack would soon learn that picking the fluffy white bolls from their cradles without including the stems was a true skill.

They all told Daddy they had picked plenty cotton in their day, but Daddy knew the dire need for work could be reason to exaggerate, but the first day in the field was all the evidence he needed. He was right about Jip Jones too; he easily picked a hefty five hundred pounds on his best days and always more than a 250–300-pound bale daily, which was average for most of the others, except the kids. They were all happy workers and sang jingles they had apparently grew up with while picking cotton… "Ah'm gonna jump down, spin around, pick a bale of cotton—jump down, turn around, pick a bale a day…"

Down by the barn, they built a big fire on Saturday nights, and we joined them. Homemade instruments, harmonica, and Daddy's mandolin would get tuned up, and everyone danced. Jip Jones was a young man with skin the color of dark chocolate, and he loved to dance. He built a platform for a small dance floor on the ground so he and others could flat-foot, a New Orleans version of buck dancing or clogging. Though Mama was expecting soon, she wanted to learn to do that. She asked Jip Jones to teach her. Everyone laughed as she lost her shyness in the fun of flat-footing. We came to love these folks. They made up songs about each other, picking cotton, and life. Jip Jones would make up silly ditties, using everyone's names in funny ways, like, "Robert der rabbit, goes jumping down der rows. He caint pick cotton and everybody knows…" He knew how to egg Robert and others into picking faster. He played right along with helping Daddy create a competitive but fun atmosphere.

By the end of the season, Dink and Robert were good cotton pickers. We would go into town and see a movie on Friday night if they picked a certain amount of cotton that week—and even if they didn't—but Mack, Lois, and I would try to pitch in to help them meet their goal. The one who picked the most got some silly prize. I believe we all inherited Daddy's competitive gene to attempt to become the fastest and best in everything we would do. When Robert and Dink complained about getting their hands pricked, Jip Jones told them, "If yo sings when yo works, yo won't pay it no mind." With long cotton bags hanging from their shoulders, they sang hymns, folk songs, and silly ditties, as they plucked the fluffy white bolls to fill them, row after row, in the Alabama sun. We sang along and learned to pick cotton and be content in dire circumstances.

When Mama's time came to have the baby, Etta Mae from the barn, who had delivered many babies, delivered ours. I guess Mama wanted to give our sister a choice of names to choose from because she named her Dorothy Evelyn Loraine, but Daddy nicknamed her "Bright Eyes" because, he said, "Her big brown eyes look like a deer's in headlights." Mama always made sure our births were recorded, but seeing Baby Bright Eyes's birth certificate is evidence that Daddy made sure the Feds would not find him through her birth in public records. He listed the daddy's name as E. Dennison, and many years later, she had a challenge getting names and date corrected.

The cotton field was picked, and the time to move on was near. Since Jip Jones had no family, Daddy asked him to go with us to find work. Daddy tried to convince Mama to let him take her and us kids to stay with Granny in Millville while he looked for work, but she refused to separate the family. We packed and left that afternoon. Daddy had made connections in Biloxi to do truck farming, but we were hardly settled in an old house way out of town when Daddy threw things together and we were on the road again. We drove through the night, and by morning, our tent was set up on the bank of the Ochlocknee River in Sopchoppy. Mama told Aunt Rhodie the rest of the story.

Mama and Aunt Rhodie continued snapping beans as they shared details of happenings since 1934. Aunt Rhodie said, "We women are like tea bags. We just don't know how strong we are until we get in hot water, do we?" They laughed, and Mama finished telling her about the tar-paper shack, Daddy getting caught, her and the jugs, and how Grandpa took us out of the woods again.

They were really enjoying each other's company, and Uncle Vester and Uncle Jim were enjoying having Daddy there to discuss politics and the weather. We kids got along good, and Mama would have meals ready on days Aunt Rhodie worked at the store. Daddy said he was working on a good deal that would be done any day, but Mama was getting antsy, feeling like we had just been imposing on them.

Robert and Mack were returning home after checking out the neighborhood and playing at the edge of the canal under the footbridge. They saw an old gentleman sitting in a chair on his porch with a brown and white beagle sitting next to him. As they approached him, Robert said, "Hello, sir."

Mack asked, "What's his name?"

The gentleman reached down and patted the dog on the head, "This here is Mr. Bones, and I'm Mr. Gibbs. You boys got names?"

Robert answered, "His is Mack and mine's Robert—Robert Meeks." He pointed to Uncle Vester's. "We're staying with our uncle down the road till Daddy finds us a place to live. Can we pet Mr. Bones?"

"He'll like that. He loves kids. Say…would you boys like to earn some money weeding my spinach patch? I could sure use some good workers."

Mama and Aunt Rhodie were doing laundry at the washtubs when the boys appeared, all excited. "Mama, we got good news."

Robert quickly added, "We got a job weeding Mr. Gibbs's spinach patch."

"Well," Mama said, "that is good news!" She teased, "Wait till I tell your Daddy tonight that you boys found a job before he did." She asked Aunt Rhodie, "Do you know this Mr. Gibbs?"

"Yes, he's a nice old man. He has that huge field of spinach down the road."

Mama asked, "With that little run-down house in the edge of the field?"

"Yes, that house is hardly bigger than an outhouse and 'bout ready to fall down. His Mama lived in it till she died quite a few years back. There's been workers staying there from time to time, but not for a while."

A few days later, when Robert reported that Mr. Gibbs's spinach was ready to be picked, Mama took off her apron and walked down the road to make a deal: we would weed and cut Mr. Gibbs's spinach if we could stay in the little house in the field until Daddy found a place for us to live. That afternoon, we moved our things into the tiny two-room house and started cutting spinach the next morning. We were hardly moved in, when Mama went into labor. Lois and I ran down the road and got Aunt Rhodie to help Dink deliver our baby. Robert and Mack were working in the spinach patch, but Lois and I stayed close to the window and listened.

Suddenly, we heard a baby cry, and Dink said, "It's another boy, Mama!"

Mama named him Jesse after our uncle. In a couple of days, Mama was back in the field, weeding and picking spinach.

A few days later, Lois and I were playing in the backyard. She went into the outhouse while I waited for her to come out. Suddenly, I heard this bloodcurdling scream. Lois burst out the door, and Mr. Gibbs's free-roaming chickens scattered everywhere. Mama came running through the spinach field, yelling, "What in the world is the matter?"

Lois was crying and pointing to the outhouse, "A stupid rooster jumped up from the back and pecked me on the bottom." She wouldn't go back into an outhouse for many years. This is my most vivid memory of living in Mr. Gibbs's spinach patch in January of 1942.

We had been there several weeks and picked a lot of spinach, when Daddy came home, excited, and told Mama, "Pack up the kids, Shorty. I found us a place to live and a good way to make a living in Pahokee."

Chapter 7

Even in the mud and scum of things, something always, always sings.
                                             —Ralph Waldo Emerson

When we crossed the railroad tracks inside Pahokee city limits, Daddy parked in front of an abandoned grocery store on the right—a big one-story wood building with a tin roof and a covered porch, built into the side of a hill and elevated on log pilings to make it level with the porch, creating a large covered area—perfect play area underneath. Steep driveways on each side of the building leveled out and ended at the edge of a canal.

We scrambled out of the car, excited to check out our new home. As I stepped upon the porch, the floor began to tremble and an earsplitting sound of a blaring train whistle and clanging bell muted our glee. The whole building shook. As the train approached, the engineer waved to us and gave an extra quick snort of the whistle. As the train passed, we waved at two hobo hitchhikers sitting in the open doorway of a box car, dangling their legs, and they waved back. When we regained our composure, our attention returned to a rusty RC Cola sign above the door of the store, another rusty Beechnut Tobacco sign over a window, and a green metal kerosene dispenser tank with a crank. Daddy opened the screen door and unlocked the other door, exposing an enormous, dusty, and dank-smelling room. The floors were uneven, with wide planks of rough lumber. Four-by-four-foot columns placed here and there supported high, open beams of the trusses that held the corrugated tin roof. On a counter by the entrance, an empty Lance Peanuts jar sat next to an old, rusty cash register showing $0.52 as its last chaching. The walls behind the cash register on the left were lined with empty shelves.

Our eyes popped when we looked to the right, as we walked in—there was a full-fledged, dust-covered soda fountain behind a bar with a row of chrome swivel stools with red round seats. The wall behind the bar was mirrored with glass shelves holding fancy glasses and dishes for sundaes and banana splits. Upon further inspection, the soda fountain had an unplugged ice cream freezer and all the works, but no ice cream. Two pale-green milkshake machines sat on a narrow counter below the glass shelves. Beyond the soda fountain, three bistro tables had skinny chairs turned upside down on top of them. We kids were giddy with joy over this find. I knew we would love our new home.

Beyond the beams, in the back of the room was a long refrigerated meat case with a glass front and a big scale, like the ones they weigh new babies on. A big area was partitioned off where, possibly, the former owners stayed. Daddy pulled back a faded, tattered green curtain covering the doorway for Mama to see. "Look here, Shorty. We can live here until we get things figured out. It has a toilet in the corner."

Mama took a deep breath and said, "I hope the water is on, Urbie, because we'll have a lot of cleaning to do. Once the kids are in school, we'll figure it out."

Mama registered Dink, Robert, Mack, and Lois for school, and they started classes. The school bus stopped right in front of our store, and I so wanted to ride that bus and go, but I wouldn't be six until after Christmas, so I had to wait another year.

We did a lot of cleaning and painting after school and on weekends. Daddy soon had the refrigerated case stocked with fish and the shelves with groceries. News of Daddy's home-smoked hams, which he had perfected years before, and wide variety of fresh fish spread fast around the Glades, so we soon had a stream of customers. Daddy spent a lot of time away from the store, meeting locals, business owners, and politicians, while Mama ran the store. We all helped. We were anxious for him to open the soda shop, but he said we had to wait until the older kids were out of school to help run it.

After closing the store at night, Daddy would give each of us money from the cash register to practice buying things and making change with each other. He had a hard time convincing Mama that teaching us how to play poker was another good way to learn math. She would not allow us to use pennies but eventually said we could use matchsticks.

We started building our three-story home behind the store. I say "we" because Daddy made sure we all helped him and the carpenters. If we were too little to swing a hammer or handle a saw, we carried boards or materials. He believed, if we could walk, we could do something. Mama pitched in to do everything she could between tending the store. She seemed happy and excited about our spacious new home. Daddy had many carpenters, and our house was finished enough for us to move in before school was out, but Mama's dream turned into a nightmare about the time we started moving in.

Mama was always calm and collected in the worst of situations, so when she went hysterical in the middle of the store after a telegram was delivered from her sister, Aunt Evelyn, I was more scared than I had ever been that June of 1942. After reading the telegram, the unfolded message fell to the floor, and she collapsed on the floor into a fetal position, screaming, "No…no…no! My daddy can't be dead!" Mack and I ran to her as she wailed like an injured animal, and Dink scooped up the paper from the floor and read it aloud, "Come home…Accident…Daddy dead…Evelyn." When she regained enough composure to talk, she gave Dink instructions to take care of us kids and the store and was on a Greyhound bus with six-month-old baby Jesse within hours.

When she returned, she made every attempt to make our new home an exciting, fun adventure, but her sadness was palpable. The bottom floor was a big open room that Daddy filled with octagon-shaped tables and chairs. He called this "the young'uns" playroom, but Mama jokingly called it "Daddy's playroom" because His friends would come and go through a door on the back side of the building to play cards every weekend, even before construction was finished.

Business was good. Daddy built a fish house between the house and canal with a big walk-in freezer and started a wholesale fish company. School was out for the summer, and true to Daddy's time and motion study program, all who were big enough to reach the cleaning counter, standing on boxes he built, were taught to scale, behead, gut, and skin fish. Of course, there was always friendly competition. Mama put her foot down on who was big enough to use sharp knives, so Daddy said I would team up with Robert and Lois with Mack. Lois and I would keep the boys supplied with fish to clean, then pack them in boxes to be iced down. Meeks Fish Company became the biggest wholesale supplier of seafood and fish for restaurants, commissaries, and fish markets in the Glades area.

As Daddy became more successful, he changed. He started dressing up more, wearing Stetson hats and Florsheim shoes, and replaced the inferior dentures he got while in prison with new ones. He changed in other ways too. Normally, years before, when he drank, he would only have one, but now he started drinking more and gambling. There was no one I'd rather be around than Daddy when he was sober, but once he had more than one drink, Dr. Jekyll turned into Mr. Hyde. He started staying away from home more, and when he did return, if he was drinking, he would be angry and physically abusive to Mama. Always, when we heard him stumbling up the stairs and crashing into furniture as he entered the house, Mama shuttled us kids into another part of the house or in a closet, but Dink and Robert would not leave Mama, so they got the brunt of his anger and abuse too.

Just before Christmas, Daddy started taking all the money from the cash drawer every night to gamble. Mama didn't usually talk to him when he was drinking, but maybe because she was seven months pregnant and knew the family's well-being was at stake, she tried to reason with him one night. She said, "Urbie, we need money to make more money. I have to make change and pay the vendors, and there's Christmas for the kids."

He started cursing and yelling at her in an angry, slurred voice—that he was working his ass off to make us a good future. Then he slapped her across the face, sending her to the floor, yelling that all she did was bitch about money and you needed money to meet the right people.

We huddled together in the closet, motionless, hearing Daddy's fury and wrath. I prayed the cursing and frightening muted sounds of Mama's attempts to quiet him would stop. He kicked Mama as he staggered past and out the door. When we heard the door slam behind him, we burst out of the closet and ran to see if Mama was okay. She wasn't—she had a swollen eye and her nose was bleeding, but she reassured us. I felt so conflicted. How could I have loved Daddy before and hate him so much that night?

We heard the engine and knew we would not see him again for a couple of days.

Mama sent us to bed, but she stayed up, frying chicken, baking sweet potatoes, and making biscuits to pack in a shoebox and paper sack. Early the next morning, we were all on a Greyhound bus, going to Granny's in Millville. Only a week had passed when Daddy came to Millville with a car full of gifts and a promise to stop drinking. He stayed in Millville a week with someone he knew, while we continued to stay with Granny. He and Mama had long talks, and he begged her to return with him. Robert and Dink were definitely against it, but once Daddy was his old self, we younger kids were glad he was there. Mama must have wanted us to be a family so bad she was willing to take another chance, because we went back with him.

Daddy filled the freezer in the soda shop with big round tubs of chocolate, vanilla, and strawberry ice cream, and the squirt containers above the tubs of ice cream with various flavors of syrups. With makings for milkshakes, sundaes, sodas, and banana splits, we were open for business. He stacked Coca-Cola boxes for Lois and me to stand on and seemed to enjoy watching all of us kids run the soda shop. I remember almost falling into the freezer while trying to dip ice cream for a milkshake.

Our brother Marion (whom Daddy nicknamed Bo) was born in Pahokee two months later.

Daddy had his own way of letting us know he loved us. He would tell his friends in our presence, "I wouldn't take a million bucks for any one of these young'uns, but I wouldn't give a plug nickel for another one"—until the next one came along. We never doubted that Daddy loved us, but his violence was confusing and frightening.

A month before we moved to Pahokee, Japan bombed Pearl Harbor and President Roosevelt declared war on Japan. Everyone seemed to stop everything they were doing and remain frozen near the radio. In spring of 1942, the War Rationing Program went into effect. First, gas and tires were rationed. Driving over thirty-five miles per hour became illegal. Soon, sugar, butter, cooking oil, meats, and many other items became rationed. The program was enforced by a volunteer rationing board, so sometimes the matter of whom you knew became important to your personal needs. There were war bond drives, and people were asked to save cans and toothpaste tubes for the war effort. Mama joined other women, making bandages for the Red Cross. We helped fill care packages to send to our service men. The sirens would ring out, warning everyone in the town to turn out lights or cover their windows to practice for air raids by the enemy. At school, kids learned all the Marine Corps, Navy, Air Force, and Coast Guard songs. Mama's brother, Uncle Hilas, joined the Army and went off to war. President Roosevelt implemented an emergency warship building program in Panama City, near Mama's hometown. That was a scary time—hearing all the sirens and talk about war and bombs.

Daddy wanted to give locals and our servicemen, when they come home on leave, a place to come to forget the war. He said our spacious store and soda shop was the perfect gathering place for all of Pahokee. Though production of jukeboxes were halted during the war and hard to come by, Daddy somehow got one he placed in middle of the store. It was loaded with 78 rpm records with all the 1940s music. I believe it cost ten cents for one song or twenty-five cents for three, but Daddy kept the music going with coins from the cash drawer. On weekend nights, the old wooden planked floors of our store bounced with dancing feet as the jukebox blared out "Chattanooga Shoe Shine Boy" and "Bugle Boy Beat" by the Andrews Sisters and "In the Mood" and "Twelfth Street Rag" by Glen Miller Band. Daddy offered ten-dollar prize for weekly jitterbug contests. Dink was a great dancer; she could have won every week, but Daddy said, "Family can't compete." Daddy and Mama loved to sing. He would lead sing-alongs with the jukebox, and we would sing "Anchors Away" when a sailor came in, or "Off We Go into the Wild Blue Yonder" if an Air Force serviceman came in. We learned all the songs on the jukebox and how to jitterbug, Charleston, juke, and do the polka. That was a scary time but some of the best memories of my childhood.

Daddy started taking long business trips. I remember when Mama drove him to Miami to catch a plane to the Bahamas to buy a fishing boat. He said he was going to supply his own catfish from Lake Okeechobee for Meeks Fish Company. We picked up two airmen and a sailor who were hitchhiking on our way to drop Daddy at the airport. They jumped in the back of the pickup with us kids. They teased us and flirted with Dink, who was fifteen. They were not much older. Jesse, who was two, observing the uniforms, said, "Sing a song."

Dink smiled, saying, "We don't know if we should sing for the sailor or the airman first."

The sailor quipped, "Well, let's flip a coin, and I choose heads," as he pulled out a nickel and flipped.

It was heads, so we started singing "Anchors Away," followed by "Off We Go into the Wild Blue Yonder."

They got a real kick out of that and gave us hugs before Mama stopped to let them out on Federal Highway in Fort Lauderdale.

Daddy bought a fancy big boat and drove it back, across the Atlantic. He first docked it in West Palm Beach, where he would sometimes stay, then moved it to Slim's Fish Camp, but I'm not sure he got to do much fishing before he lost it in a poker game.

Just when we thought the drinking and abuse was behind us, the abuse would start all over again. Mama, Dink, and Robert were the ones who bore the brunt of Daddy's ire, but I clearly remember the one time we younger ones were involved. I remember in late 1942, he staggered in from a night of drinking, cleaned out the cash drawer, and stomped into the living room where we were doing homework and Mama was sewing. He accused Mama of lying about how much money the store and fish company made that day. He slapped her around and asked Robert, "Did you take any money out of that cash drawer?"

Robert said, "No, sir, I didn't."

Saying he'd get the truth out of one of us, he whipped off his belt and called us by name, "Buzz, Lois, Mack, Robert, Dink, get up here!" We lined up, and he started swinging the belt, leaving welts on one, then the next…all down the line. We were afraid to run or move. Though Mama was pregnant, when she stepped between him and us to stop him, he slung her against the wall and started hitting her with the belt. Robert, fourteen, ran and got Daddy's loaded gun that we were not allowed to touch. He pointed it at Daddy and screamed, "Daddy, don't hit her again, or I'll kill you and spend the rest of my life in prison!" Daddy looked dazed as he gazed at Robert pointing the gun at him. He shook his head, as if to wake up, dropped the belt, and staggered out the door and back downstairs. Dink went into the store and called the police. Daddy knew all the police and sheriffs personally, so when the officer who came told him, "Urbie,

Daddy with kids, Pahokee

you need to come with me for tonight and sleep it off," he went.

When Robert mumbled "That son of a bitch" and Dink said "He's crazy, Mama," she shook her head and said, "Okay, kids, listen to me. He shouldn't have done that, but that's your daddy and I don't want to hear you talk about him like that!"

Robert started to say something, and she added, "He's working some things out after some bad times of his own."

Mama knew they would let him out the next morning, so she woke us up before daylight and drove Daddy's truck to the Greyhound station where she left it, and we all boarded the first bus north with a shoebox filled with food and a pillowcase with diapers and clothes.

Mama had just learned she was expecting again and not feeling very well, but she played along with guessing games to entertain us. The weather was miserably hot in the non-air-conditioned bus, so she opened her window and removed her shoes from her swollen feet. Baby Jesse grabbed one of her shoes and tossed it out the open window of the bus as it sped down the highway. A young airman named Everette Blanton, returning from leave, was sitting across the aisle next to Dink and saw what happened. Later, when the bus stopped to pick up passengers in Tampa where he was stationed, he said something to the driver and jumped off the bus and ran into a store across from the bus station. The driver waited a few minutes after passengers were loaded. The airman returned, jumped back on the bus, and handed a pair of bedroom slippers to Mama, probably the only shoes he could afford. She tried to pay him, but he wouldn't take her money. He jumped off the waiting bus and waved to us as the bus drove away.

We were at Granny's a short time, when Mama heard about President Roosevelt implementing the Emergency Ship-Building Program. With the shortage of men due to the war, Wainwright Shipyard in Panama City, several miles from Millville, had switched from riveting ships to welding and were training and hiring women to weld. She applied for a job and was hired and trained to tact-weld warships, earning forty dollars a week. Seeing old war posters of "Rita the Riveter" always brings flashbacks of Mama going to work with welding helmet in hand, her long, thick black hair tied up under a bandanna, and dressed in her brother's clothes who was away in the Army.

We started school in Millville but were not there two months when Daddy drove up in a new car and told Mama, "I've definitely quit drinking this time, and I'm working on building a real nice restaurant with my friend Bose Levins. He owns the Beach Club on the Ocean in Singer Island." He somehow convinced Mama that things would be different, and we all ate hamburgers in a restaurant on the way back to Pahokee and had a fun trip home.

Chapter 8

*In the end, everything will be okay. If it's not
okay, It's not yet the end.*
—Fernando Sabino, translated from Portuguese

We returned with Daddy to Pahokee, with Mama's faith that this just
might be the answer—running a restaurant where the whole family
would work together. She loved to cook and envisioned how great
working together would be, but when Mama learned more details
about the "restaurant," I'm sure red lights were flashing in her head. It
would be called the Club Savoy. It would be a "restaurant"—but inside
a nightclub with gambling tables in a back room. This must have given
her reason to pause, but given how excited and determined he was to
build the nicest high-end nightclub and restaurant in the Glades, she
told Dink, "Maybe this is what he needs to make him feel good about
himself. With Bose Levins, a very successful and respected businessman
as a partner, I'm sure there are things they can learn from each other."

Daddy had either sold Meeks Fish Company, or lost it gambling,
but he restocked the shelves and refrigerated case in the store with groceries and fish. We didn't reopen the soda shop because it had not been
profitable. I suppose we kids had something to do with that, but we still
had the jukebox to sing and dance to. We spent a lot of time playing
under the store, when we weren't in school, doing homework, or helping Mama. Lois and I, now eight and ten, were responsible for keeping
Bright Eyes, Jesse, and Bo within the confines of our yard, and though
we weren't allowed to leave the yard, Lois and I would sneak out to the
tracks, place pennies on the rails, and sneak back to retrieve the flat-
tened ones after the train passed. Those times were fun and peaceful.

One thing after another was holding up Daddy's project. After a difficult time getting permits, they hit a bigger snag. Almost everything was rationed in 1944 during the war. They obtained permits but couldn't get building materials to build. Through their many connections, they knew bars, restaurants, and gambling houses couldn't get delivery of liquor either. Clergymen, policemen, and a few others were allotted unlimited gas ration stamps, but liquor salesmen were only allowed three gallons per week, hardly enough to get them out of Miami or Jacksonville where distribution centers were located. When they learned Ben Danbaum, a former head of Omaha's Detective Investigative Bureau, with extensive contacts, had opened the distribution center for Lord Calvert in Miami, they made a deal. Daddy knew everyone in the Glades: locals, business owners, politicians, and lawmen. He somehow secured enough gas ration stamps for Ben Danbaum's liquor salesmen, and he and Bose Levins were put in contact with a lumber company out west to buy lumber. Construction was under way.

In May of 1944, Daddy's friend John Kirk from Belle Glade threw his hat in the ring to run for sheriff of Palm Beach County for 1945. Since that day, Daddy's time and energy was totally absorbed between building a nightclub and campaigning for Kirk. He totally abandoned the store and his family, but Mama hoped this cause would help him come to terms with his demons. Daddy knew John Kirk since John first moved to Pahokee in 1928 and worked his way up from police officer to constable in that district, to chief of police in Belle Glade, to constable of the Eighth District in 1932—an office he still held. Of course, A candidate from the Glades was a joke to all the big-shot politicians in the West Palm Beach area—to think a hick from the Glades thinks he could ever win an election against the incumbent, Sheriff Jack Baker—or *any* candidate from the coast. No one from the Glades had ever won an election for a major county office. The Baker family had controlled the sheriff's office most of the years since 1909, and they knew Baker would not lose to this hick. Daddy became obsessed with making sure he did just that! He wanted to avenge the Bakers for the way they killed John Ashley (of the infamous Ashley Gang) and his men—not that they didn't deserve being caught by the law for robbing banks, killing a lawman in a shoot-out, and other egregious acts—but Daddy vehemently opposed the way they did it. He heard from locals that when Baker and his deputies ambushed them on a bridge and shot them in November of 1924, Ashley and his men were handcuffed. Daddy was good friends with the Upthegrove family whose daughter, Laura, known as "The Queen of the Everglades," was John Ashley's girlfriend. Daddy had campaigned for Woody and Dewitt Upthegrove, and he knew John Ashley's daddy, Joe, who had been killed in a shoot-out at a moonshine camp by the Bakers. Joe and his family controlled the moonshine in the area when Daddy first came to the Glades in early 1924, but Joe, unlike his son, was a good man who always helped family, friends, and neighbors who were less well-off and spent a lot of moonshine money for the community. Many of the locals were still upset with the way things were handled by the sheriff and his deputies.

Daddy was a man on a big mission to get Kirk elected, to see the blacks he registered cast their votes safely, and to put an end to the poll tax, the literacy tests, and the rein of the Baker family in Palm Beach County.

*****

Every time we thought things were getting better, the abuse would start all over again. He started coming home after drinking at political events, being verbally and physically abusive. One night he came home after midnight and was cursing Mama because she had stashed the money from the cash drawer. He was furious, but he was so drunk she was able to dodge any serious blows, and she didn't give him the money. He fell over a chair, and Mama locked us kids and herself in a bedroom. He was up and gone by daylight. No matter how much he drank, or how little he slept, he was always up and out by the time the sun came up. He didn't return home for almost a week, and when he returned, he was in a good mood. He had been campaigning in West Palm Beach and was feeling confident John Kirk could win the election. He told Mama he had gone to see his friend Cracker Johnson, a colored man who lived in West Palm Beach. He was a millionaire who owned a bar and lots of downtown real estate. Cracker Johnson was well respected by everyone who had any standing in town, including black and white business leaders, politicians, and lawmen. Cracker Johnson once loaned the City of West Palm Beach $50,000 to help the city make payroll and keep its doors open. He was known to have earned his millions from rum-running and moonshine during Prohibition, and he bought up a lot of real estate in West Palm Beach during the land bust in the midtwenties. Daddy was sure he had his support and help in getting Kirk elected.

Daddy bounced between construction of the club and campaigning, and when he was in town, he continued to clean out the cash drawer. Mama knew it was only a matter of time before she could not keep the store running. She was expecting again and was determined to find a way to make ends meet and manage to keep us together without bouncing us back and forth to Granny's.

The Club Savoy opened on October 3, 1944, and John Kirk won his election in November, sending shock waves through Palm Beach County's West Palm Beach aristocrats—many who attended the huge celebration at the biggest and newest upper-class nightclub in the Glades. John Kirk was sheriff of Palm Beach County until 1960, when he was charged with taking bribes from gambling interests. He wasn't prosecuted, but he retired after fifteen years in office.

In February, Mama went into labor with her tenth baby. Daddy wanted her to have the baby in the hospital like his friends' wives, but she wanted to have her midwife deliver it. She agreed to have the baby in the hospital to please him. When her pains were getting close together, she called Dr. Spooner, who met her at the Pahokee hospital. She gave birth and came home on the third day, but our baby sister, Bobby Jean, would remain in the hospital a week because she almost died with double pneumonia. Mama swore she would never go to a hospital to have a baby again. She declared, the next one would be at home with a midwife, where there were no germs.

Daddy always enjoyed taking us kids with him to the club when he was working on paperwork or checking on something during the day. He allowed us to drink sodas, clink on the piano, play the jukebox, and dance around the elevated dance floor, while employees cleaned and prepared for the night's business. We got to know the bartender, Ms. Dixie, who was very nice. She was a large lady with bright-red hair, wore lots of makeup and jewelry, and was lots of fun. She played the ukulele and told jokes. She was teaching me how to play and sing "If you like a ukulele lady" and told me if I would remember how to play two songs and sing them for her, she would buy me my own ukulele. I practiced and practiced in the corner every time I went to the club with Daddy. I was nervous, but I really wanted that uke, so I finally sang and played the two songs she taught me, and she said, "You can keep that ukulele." I will always have fond memories of Ms. Dixie and time spent at the Club Savoy.

I often went with Daddy to deliver rolls of tickets to the colored juke joints on the outskirts of towns where the coloreds could go after dark. Coloreds were not allowed to be in the city limits after dark. He would tell me, "Now don't tell your mama where we went, or she won't let you go with me anymore." I learned years later we were delivering Bolita tickets, an illegal form of gambling that came from Cuba, which was—and still is—popular with the poorest people. *Bolita* means "little ball." Like the balls with numbers on them for lotto. The coloreds were always real fun and nice to me. They would offer me sodas and a pickled pig's foot from a big jar that sat on the bars of all the juke joints in the Glades. While looking at archives of photos commissioned by the federal government to capture life during the Depression and war in the Glades, I was shocked to recognize a photo of one of the places I had been in many times with Daddy.

Daddy gambled the profits from the store. Mama was always optimistic and hoping he would change, but his gambling persisted. When she couldn't restock or pay the electric bill, she knew she had to do something. Though she was weary, she always had a lot of starting-over power and determination. She closed the store and packed all of us in the truck and drove to Hudgins' Fish Company in West Palm Beach, where Daddy bought wholesale, and asked to set up a credit account. Bill Hudgins knew Mama would be good for it. We returned with boxes filled with iced-down mullet, catfish, and sheephead fish and peddled them in the colored projects and migratory camps. As Mama drove slowly through the camps, Lois and I would ring a cowbell from the bed of the truck as we sang out the ditty we made up for the occasion: "Here comes the fish-man, fish-man, fish-man...Get out your dish-pan, dish-pan, dish-pan...Come here, and buy your fish till we come again." She would stop the truck when tired farm workers staggered out of their little tin-roofed shacks toward our truck. Mack would jump out from the cab and hang the scale on the hook he rigged on the bed of the truck. Lois and I would hold the fish in the air for their approval, and Mack would weigh it and tell them "how much," usually less than the scale showed if they had kids with them and didn't have enough money. He'd say, "I think I made a mistake, let me reweigh that." He learned this from Daddy in the store.

Things seemed to have calmed down with Daddy, so we were very shocked when he came home one night and announced we were going to be moving to Belle Glade. He said he had a new project there. The truth was that he had lost everything we owned gambling at his own gambling house. We were in for another one of "Daddy's big adventures."

One day we were living in a nice home, and the next day, we were homeless. He told us we were going on a new adventure, that he was going to build a new store in Belle Glade.

Juke Joint
(photo by Marion Post Wolcott)

Chapter 9

Attitude is the difference between ordeal and adventure.

—Bob Bitchin

Right after John Kirk won the election in 1945, we moved into vacant migrant housing in the edge of a cane field on the outskirts of Belle Glade. Daddy hauled water from town for cooking, and we caught rainwater to wash our hair, but Mama strained canal water through a diaper and boiled it to take baths. We used kerosene lamps for light, and Mama cooked on a kerosene stove again. Robert and Mack replaced glass in the windows that were broken or missing in the three rooms we claimed. The only other people living there were a man who worked for the prison, his wife, and their daughter. They lived at the opposite end of the row of attached rooms from us. The daughter's name was Debra. She was Bright Eyes's age. She had curly blond hair and blue eyes and owned a Shetland pony named Baby. I thought she was the prettiest and luckiest girl I had ever known. She was a member of the 4-H Club at Belle Glade Elementary, and she allowed us to ride her pony.

Daddy drove us into town to register for our new school. We walked a mile out to the main road to catch the school bus each morning. Debra walked out to the road to catch the bus with us, but she wasn't allowed to come into our rooms. When we told Daddy we wanted our own pony, he said, "You're lucky you have sisters and brothers to play with. Now, let me ask you, would you rather have all your sisters and brothers, or only a pony to play with?" At times, that would have been a no-brainer, but we were convinced we should feel sorry for her.

Debra's mama stayed to herself, and Mama wasn't one to impose herself on new acquaintances, so they didn't become friends right away. Until one day we heard Debra's mama screaming bloody murder. Mama ran down to their place, with us following, to see what was wrong. A snake had invaded their kitchen, and Debra's mama was on top of the table, jumping up and down, screaming. Mama had always been deathly afraid of snakes, but she was always brave in emergencies. She told us, "Get back. Get back!" as she grabbed the broom by their door and chased the snake out. Mama and Debra's mama became friends after that.

Daddy spent a lot of time away from home. He told Mama he was working on starting a new business and getting us a nice place to live. He told us we'd be moving into our new home soon. He took us all into town and showed us some vacant land with a pulley sawmill set up on the back of it. Strings tied to pegs in the ground showed us where the walls of our home would be. He said, "Yep, we will soon be living above the best grocery store and butcher shop in the Glades." He unrolled several big sheets of plans he had drawn and spread them on the hood of the car to show Mama. She bit her lower lip as she looked and said nothing. The land was near downtown and a block from the ice house and Royal's Dry Good Store. The property faced Fourth Street that ran through the middle of colored town. I hoped we'd be living in town soon. I didn't like living without electricity or running water, and I was deathly afraid of snakes.

Daddy and Ithaniel, our half brother, who was a skilled block layer and plaster, started construction. Daddy sawed big logs for lumber needed for the beams and foundation, and Ithaniel would supervise, lay concrete block, and do the plastering. Most of the first floor would be our grocery store and butcher shop with a small part leased to Sasser's Glass Company. We would live above the store in the biggest and nicest apartment in the front. The remaining apartments would be rented for income. We would be living within walking distance to the movie theater, and only a few blocks, crossing a footbridge to get to school.

Mama was anxious for us to make new friends and enjoy our new school and activities. Daddy didn't want Mack to get involved with extracurricular activities. He tried to convince her that Mack's time would be better spent learning a usable skill from his brother than in a classroom. Mama put her foot down, and Mack stayed in school. Mack liked school and was a good student. He and Lois placed in the top ten at the county spelling bee the next year, but being of slight build and rather introverted, I believe he was more comfortable around people and things he knew. He said he was not interested in getting knocked around on the football field, and when Mama suggested he should consider joining the band, he said, "No thanks, Mama, I'll just stick to my harmonica." Consequently, Mack became a good block layer and plasterer.

Daddy hired more help, and the building was going up fast. We were all anxious to move into town, but Mama wouldn't go until the railings around the porches that wrapped three sides of the second floor were in place. We finally moved into an unfinished apartment, in an unfinished upstairs, over an unfinished grocery store and butcher shop that was stocked and opened for business. The railings were in but not painted. No problem. Daddy had enough green paint for the top rail and white for the spindles to cover the whole town and keep us kids busy for a long time. We had electricity and running water in all the apartments. There was a room under the stairs on both sides of the store, each with a flush toilet, a lavatory, and a shower to be shared by us and tenants. We were happy to leave the cane field and to put the kerosene stove and lamps away, but we felt bad leaving Debra and Baby out there all alone with no sisters and brothers.

Mama took care of the store and meat market while the guys worked on the many unfinished areas. She kept baby Bobby Jean, who was a year old, and Bo and Jesse, three and five, with her in the store while we were in school. After school, Bright Eyes, Lois, and I helped in the store and watched the younger ones. One day, after school, Lois and I were supposed to be watching Bo and Jesse while they finished their naps upstairs. We were playing jacks and didn't realize Bo was awake and had wandered into the vacant apartment with no flooring. He fell through the Celetex ceiling of the store below, onto the concrete floor of the meat market, and was knocked unconscious. Mama said she almost fainted when she saw him plummeting from the ceiling from the front of the store. She screamed for Daddy as she ran to the back and picked him up. Bo was out cold, and Mama and Daddy rushed him to the doctor. He regained consciousness on the way to the doctor's office, but he had a concussion, and we had to keep him awake and watch him closely. I prayed really hard until I knew he was okay. Lois and I were much better babysitters after that. Later, our brothers often teased him about being dropped on his head.

Not long after Bo fell through the ceiling, Daddy bought an attachment for the hamburger grinding machine to make his own sausage and hot dogs. He was teaching Mack how to make "the best sausage in the Glades." He was chopping meat on the butcher block behind Mack, as he was telling him about his secret spices. Mack was feeding meat into the machine with a wooden paddle to be ground while he listened. He knew he would be expected to make sausage on his own after the lesson. When he pushed a chunk of meat into the grinder with his finger that the paddle missed, he yelped, "Damn, so-no-va-bitch!" He jerked his bleeding hand out, leaving the end of his finger with the ground meat in the sausage skin. As blood spewed from his finger all over his and Daddy's white aprons, Daddy grabbed his hand, washed it under the faucet, wrapped it in a butcher apron, and rushed him to the doctor. Mama was upset that Daddy didn't grind the meat and let Mack cut the links or do something less dangerous. Daddy teased Mama, as he rustled Mack's hair, "Mack not only messed up his right hand for a while. He messed up a batch of the best sausage in the Glades."

After that, things seemed calm for a while. Daddy stayed busy finishing the apartments and keeping things going—butchering cows and hogs, cutting the meats, and smoking hams. He was pleased folks from Pahokee were driving eleven miles to Belle Glade to buy his hams and smoked pork chops. He was home more than usual, and his drinking seemed to be in control, but everyone was waiting for the next shoe to drop. I finished the second grade, and Lois finished the fourth grade in our new school. What I remember most about school that year was how we had to line up along the wall in the hall and hold our arm out to get a shot when we reached the nurse sitting at a desk. I was afraid of needles and wanted to run to the back of the line when I got close, but Mama said I needed to be brave so the younger kids wouldn't get scared. She said all the kids had to get shots to go to school, and I sure wanted to go to school.

Daddy with fish, Belle Glade

One night in July of 1946, Daddy came home very upset at the news that his friend James Jerome "Cracker" Johnson had been shot and killed the night before. He said Cracker Johnson was attacked behind his own bar in West Palm Beach, and one of two attackers shot him. The rumor was that they were hired by a white mob who wanted him stopped having so much influence in Palm Beach County. Mama was afraid Daddy would go on a binge, but he didn't; he just kept shaking his head and saying Cracker Johnson's life was a terrible, terrible loss for a lot of people. After his funeral, the *Palm Beach Post* reported that his funeral had standing-room only, with hundreds of people, both black and white, who came to bury their king. Daddy said, "The black community lost their best friend."

Daddy took over collecting the rents and the money from the cash register at the store. He wasn't smoking enough hams to meet demand and began staying away a few days at a time. Mama was expecting again in a few weeks. About a week after his friend died, he told Mama he had a good idea; he rented our apartment out to someone who would take care of the store until after she had the baby. He said, since the kids were out of school for the summer, we could camp out in the little house that was on the property where we had our hog pens in Chosen. He added, "It's just down the road from Slim's Fish Camp and the lake. The kids can spend the summer fishing, swimming and boating."

Mama said, "Urbie, that place is a run-down, bug-filled shack," but he said it was a good shelter for camping and would be good for the young'uns.

Mama was afraid of getting Daddy fired up again, so we got things together for a campout and went to the shack. Dink was beyond furious. She took a job at Ted's Sweet Shop across town and rented a room above it. Mama was sad but gave her an extra-long hug when she moved out. Robert was chomping at the bit to leave too. When his attempt to join the Army failed because he was only sixteen, he moved in with Dink. Dink helped us clean the place before we moved in then decided to stay with Mama until she had the baby, so she could help the midwife.

The following week, Mama went into labor, and Dink and a midwife delivered a beautiful, towheaded, blue-eyed baby girl by our hog pens in Chosen on July 16, 1947. We named her Shirley Ann, but Daddy named her Lulu. He disappeared, but Dink stayed.

When the baby was three days old, Dink told Mama, "Daddy's gambling friends may not know it, but they are moving." She went to see them and told them, "My mama is living in a tiny two-room shack with eight kids, including a new baby, and you have to move." They said they paid Daddy rent and made a deal with him. She told them to find Daddy and get their money back, because the deal was off. They didn't move until Dink started throwing their things over the banister. They didn't have much to throw, because our furniture and things were still there. We lived in fear, expecting Daddy to come home in a rage. He returned a few nights after we moved back, cold sober. He told Mama, "We're going on the adventure of a lifetime."

Mama said, "It doesn't make sense to me, Urbie. Who's taking care of the store while we are gone?" Daddy said we would close for the summer. He told her he learned through the Bureau of Farm Workers there was a shortage of cherry pickers in Michigan, and he thought the adventure could be fun and educational for the kids to see new places and do new things. He called to inquire before we left Florida and learned the season had started, but they still needed pickers. No one wanted to ask Mama, but I think we all knew we had lost our home again—before it was even completely built.

In a couple of days, we were loading an army tent and camping gear in the trunk of a 1936 Chevrolet sedan Daddy recently bought. We piled in on top of each other and meandered north to Michigan.

We drove for four days to get there because Daddy said we needed to take it easy. We stopped along the way to picnic and stretch our legs, and sometimes Daddy had to work on the car. We slept along the roadsides, in the car and under the tent draped from the top of the car to the ground.

Along the roadways, we noticed there were more cars than before that were not black. We made a game out of counting them. We read Burma-Shave signs: "If these signs blur and bounce around, you better park and walk to town." We made up our own silly ones, but Mama told us, "I think they are supposed to be about shaving cream." We worked on it: "Dress up good and shave your face, so you won't be your wife's disgrace." We soon tired of that and started making up silly songs.

We finally arrived in Bear Lake, Michigan, where we pitched our big tent under a maple tree across the road from the farmhouse of the Hansen Brothers, who owned the cherry orchards we would be working in. Chester Hansen and his wife were older and had never had kids. I believe they were fascinated with us having so many. They were unbelievably nice to us. They allowed us kids to ride their work-horses, help drive the cows to the barn, and even pick apples and pears in their private fruit orchard next to their house. I thought Daddy was going to kill Mack when he climbed an apple tree and broke a branch. They couldn't believe we had never seen an apple, pear, or cherry tree before. They laughed when we asked them if they had ever seen an orange tree. They hadn't—they had never been out of Michigan, and we had never been out of Florida until then. The Hansens also got a good laugh from Daddy showing off our three-year-old brother's political savvy. He asked our youngest brother, Bo, "Now, when we're in Florida, what are you?"

Bo would answer, "I'm a dim-o-cat."

And then, "When you're in Michigan, what are you?" To which he would answer, "I'm a we-pup-a-can."

The first of picking was in full swing. Five kids from a Catholic family who lived locally were at the orchard with other pickers. They picked cherries each summer to pay for their school clothes. They had a nice home and a small farm not too far away. Their Daddy worked their farm, and their Mama stayed home with the younger kids who were too young to pick. We were nervous, afraid of making fools of ourselves, but Daddy told us, "Just watch the kids to see how they pick, and we'll find a faster, better way. Before long, you'll be the best pickers in the orchard and leave them all in the dust."

There was a pile of harnesses that looked like equipment for a big dog, next to several stacks of empty buckets. We watched them put their arms into the harnesses and attach the handle of a bucket, leaving the bucket hanging in front of them, hands-free. They grabbed a stack of empty buckets and proceeded to the first tree in the row. We did the same and claimed the row of trees next to theirs. We observed how they raked the clusters of cherries into the bucket in front of them. We kept an eye on how many full buckets were on the ground under their tree and tried to fill more buckets than them. We followed them with our full buckets to the trailer where Mr. Hansen's nephew Chum Hill dumped the cherries into a bin and gave the empty buckets back with a ticket for each bucket of cherries. The Showalters told us to hang on to those tickets to turn in at the end of the day for money.

A fierce competition developed between the Meeks and Showalter kids. I believe we were responsible for increasing their production, for sure. They were not as competitive as us, but they agreed that working was more fun when we were racing and singing. By the end of the season, between all of us, we had all the pickers singing in rounds with us or requesting songs.

At first, we took all the kids to the orchard, until we were familiar with our surroundings. We older ones helped Mama with the younger ones. Daddy picked with Mack, Lois, Bright Eyes, and me from the ladders while Jesse, six, and Mama picked from the branches near the ground and watched Bo and Bobby Jean, while Baby Lulu played on a quilt in the playpen Daddy made.

Almost every day after work, we older kids raced a mile over a ridge of wildflowers behind the Hansens' barn to Lake Michigan for baths. We would always welcome a cold drink when we reached the beach where there was a pipe with cold water flowing 24-7 from an artesian well. "Old Facefull" was scratched in the hardened pad of concrete that held the pipe that spewed the fresh spring water into the air for the pleasure of sunbathers or nearby workers. The lake was icy cold, and the soap almost froze to our washcloth, but it could be refreshing if we jumped around in the water and kept moving after a long day in the orchard. Our friends' mama would sometimes drive them to meet us at the lake, bringing a basket of fresh-picked corn, a huge pot, and a big bowl of home-churned butter, and we would gather driftwood for a fire and have a corn roast on the beach.

We became close friends with the Showalter family and hated to leave them, but nights were getting colder in the tent, and we Florida Crackers began to long for warmer weather. We said goodbye to them and the Hansen Brothers and packed up to return home to start school the day after Labor Day. We became good cherry pickers and were invited to return the next summer. Daddy beamed when Chester Hansen told him, "I can't believe children that young can pick cherries like yours can." Daddy was proud; his "time and motion" training was working.

We picked tomatoes in Indiana on the way home and were glad to leave the tomato fields to go home—wherever that would end up being.

Chapter 10

When you can tell your story and it doesn't make you cry, you know you have healed.
—Author unknown

When we overheard Daddy telling Mama we wouldn't be going back to Fourth Street, Lois quickly asked, "Daddy, where will we live?"

He said, "I got a surprise for you young'uns and your Mama. You'll see." We drove right through the middle of Belle Glade on Main Street, in the little agricultural town we had left. We turned at Jack's Fish Market onto Fifth Street and hardly drove a block, when he pulled into the wide dirt driveway of a big, old two-story wood-frame apartment house on the right. The paint was peeling and weeds surrounded it, but it had glass in the windows, unlike the place where we lived in the cane field. When he parked, Mama looked pale; she shrugged her shoulders and shook her head in disbelief. "Urbie, don't even think…"

This was where Uncle Fletcher and his family lived, and I think Mama thought Daddy wanted us to move in with them.

He interrupted her, "Shorty, it's not what you think. Fletcher and his family don't own this anymore, because we do, and I wanted to surprise you. This place will be a good fixer-upper…and plenty room for your garden." Daddy nodded toward the apartments, tilted his head, and asked, "Well, what do you think?"

We kids jumped out and scattered in all directions to explore our new home, but she sat there looking at him and said, "Urbie, sometimes what you call a 'fixer-upper' could more accurately be called a 'disaster.'" But she got out of the car, and with Lulu on her hip, she walked to the door of the apartment behind him, hesitating on the step. Daddy wrapped his arm over her shoulder and happily pointed out the changes he would make to create our new home. Biting her lip, she listened as she looked around and nodded her head slowly.

I was never sure of how Daddy acquired the property. Possibly, Uncle Fletcher owed him money, because Daddy was always loaning, or giving, money to relatives. He gave our half sister Luvera and her family money to move from Tallahassee and open a store down the road from our store across town, and I've heard through the family grapevine that he helped finance his brother John and his son Lambert's move from North Florida to the Glades, where they, too, opened grocery stores.

We soon learned all about creosoting timbers, building porches, painting bannisters, and putting on a new roof. Daddy had us all working, and we soon had porches where there were none—on the first and second floors of the front, right, and back sides of the building. Interior steps to second floor were removed to create more living area, and a stairway to the second floor was rerouted to the porch on the side. Removing interior walls of three apartments, he made a big apartment for us with three bedrooms, a large living room, a dining area, and a small kitchen. Though the icebox would require a three-block walk daily to the ice house for a ten-cent block of ice, we had running water and electric. We felt like we were in high cotton.

Eventually, other apartments were refurbished and soon rented to mostly crew bosses working in the packing houses and fields of surrounding farms.

Once we finished the apartments, Daddy was seldom home. He said he was working on finding a way to make more money. He would occasionally allow people who were hard on their luck, as he called it, to have free rent, and sometimes when he did collect rent—and gambled it in backrooms of local juke joints—he would say, "That's the best way to get acquainted with the locals."

I couldn't figure out why we had to leave our home and soda shop in Pahokee, or our nice home over the store and butcher shop on Fourth Street, but I was relieved to have a home again. Once Mama got over the initial shock of possibly living with Uncle Fletcher, I could tell she was happy that unlike the shack in Chosen, our nice home in Pahokee, or the last home on Fourth Street, she now had plenty of rich black muck for a garden.

With our help, she planted a big garden in the back and had Daddy build chicken coops and a henhouse on the side of our backyard, between the house and garden. The chicken coops were soon filled with peeps of baby chicks. We planted pole beans, okra, eggplant, scallions, lettuce, tomatoes, turnips, collards, and mustard greens. Thanks to the warm climate and "black gold" in the Glades—known as the Winter Vegetable Capital of America—in six months we were feasting on fresh vegetables and fried chicken, and our baby chicks became laying hens and crowing roosters, followed by more baby peeps. Daddy planted a grapefruit and papaya tree on a small spot of ground on the right of the drive. He budded orange and tangerine branches onto the grapefruit tree to get grapefruit, oranges, and tangerines from it and called it his "ambrosia" tree.

We kids gathered bunches of collards and mustard greens and sold them door-to-door for twenty-five cents a bunch in the nearby housing projects. Mama eventually had enough profits from our garden, chickens, and eggs, stashed in a tie-bag under her mattress to buy a milk cow. She was reluctant to give the money to Daddy for fear he would gamble it or disappear on a binge, but how else could we get our cow? Several days passed with no sign of a cow. He told Mama, "I'm still looking for just the right one." Mama was worried he had spent the money, but on the fourth day, as Lois and I were playing jacks on the front porch, we were startled by the blast of Uncle Vester's truck horn as Daddy drove into the front yard. "Beep-beep-beep-beep-beep—beep, beep!" Mama emerged through the front screen door, wiping her hands on her apron, and our siblings appeared from different directions. Daddy stepped from the truck and, pointing both hands at the back of the truck, said, "Tah-dah!" Behind the wooden slats attached to the sides and back of the truck was a beautiful golden tan Jersey milk cow looking at us with huge, curious brown eyes. Surprised, Mama covered her mouth with both hands, as she stepped closer and gave Daddy a hug.

Daddy pounded a metal stake into the ground of the grassy vacant field across the dirt road from us. Mama tied a rope around our cow's neck and attached it securely to the stake. It was love at first sight between Mama and her beautiful Jersey cow.

After much debate, we kids agreed on the name Lilly for our cow; however, Daddy had already named her Bessie. Mama would say, "Urbie, stop calling her Bessie. That's not the least bit funny," but Daddy would just laugh and say, "That name fits her." He loved teasing Mama. You see, Mama had a friend named Bessie, a very large woman with humongous bosoms, who lived nearby. Mama was very fond of her, and we kids loved her. She took in washing and would help Mama in exchange for vegetables from our garden. We didn't understand the inside joke, but when he again referred to our cow as Bessie, Mama said, "Urbie, you've got to stop it! You now have the kids calling that cow Bessie."

A few days later, Mama's friend Bessie and she were sitting at the big homemade table, drinking sweet tea and shelling black-eyed peas to be canned. She caught Mama looking at her from across the table. She looked up with her big dark eyes and, slowly shaking her head from side to side, as she flashed her white teeth in a broad smile, said, "Ms. Leila, don't you worry none 'bout Mr. Urbie naming yo cow my name. It don't bother me none. It rather pleases me, 'cause I knows yo chil'ren loves me jest like they loves that cow." Before long, Mama was calling our cow Bessie.

I loved going to the pasture to milk Bessie with Mama or my brother Mack every morning before breakfast as the sun came up and every afternoon before supper. After each milking, Mama would skim the cream off the top and pour it into mason jars to save until there was enough to make butter. After ten glasses were half filled with warm milk for each of us, she poured the rest into mason jars and added vinegar to make buttermilk for her world-class biscuits, or to be poured over chunks of cornbread for Daddy and my brothers' favorite snack. When there was enough cream collected, we kids took turns chugging the wood paddle up and down in our old pottery churn. As the cream shish-sloshed, it got thicker and thicker, until it transformed into a delectable, spreadable mass the color of the sun.

Homemade butter still creates fond memories of Mama's hot biscuits and our beloved Bessie, but my siblings and I still cringe remembering Mama making us drink warm milk.

*****

When the 1948 elections heated up, Daddy became heavily involved in politics again. There was a little wooden platform set up on Main Street, with red, white, and blue banners draped around it, and Daddy insisted on us kids going with him to listen to every politician who came to town. He had us deliver flyers from door to door all over town. He wanted to make sure John Kirk got reelected as sheriff and Dewitt Upthegrove, formerly from Pahokee, got reelected as supervisor of elections in Palm Beach County. He had fought hard to get them elected in 1944—Kirk to be the first from the Glades, and Upthegrove, who lived in West Palm Beach, but grew up in Pahokee, to win major county elections. Daddy wanted to make sure they would not be the last.

He was campaigning hard in the Glades and other parts of the county. Some people involved lived in a couple of our apartments. There were always people coming and going and having meetings there. I'm not sure if this had anything to do with what happened next.

Life was very good; we were enjoying school and our new home. Rows of colorful mason jars filled with beans, corn, tomatoes, and black-eyed peas lined the walls of our little kitchen, and pretty curtains Mama made enhanced our living area. Daddy even set up a wash house for Mama in the back with an older wringer washer he brought home. It only worked for a short time, but Mama had the thrill—for the first time in her life—of giving her scrub board and knuckles a rest. We had a mahogany piano in the living room across from Mama's pedal sewing machine, and life was very good…until it wasn't.

In March, Daddy made a deal to acquire the dilapidated, run-down property next door. It had an L-shaped building of attached motel-like rooms and a boarded-up run-down building in front that was once a grocery store. The rooms each had a door and tiny window with a single lightbulb dangling from the center of the ceiling. They were occupied by migrant workers who labored in the black muck fields, picking beans in the blazing Everglades sun. At night, they spent their meager, hard-earned money on wine to dull their bleak existence. Mama called the place "the wino camp," and she didn't allow us to cross the dirt road on the side of our apartments that separated us from the wino housing. All the rooms faced a bathhouse that stood between the row of rooms and the boarded-up front building. The front building had two rooms, each with a toilet, lavatory, and shower stall. The rows of rooms had no inside water, so the tenants all shared the bathhouse.

Soon, Daddy had us moving Mama's sewing machine and our beds into the abandoned grocery store in front of the line of rooms. Walls separating our bedrooms in the apartment were replaced with quilts hanging from the low ceiling in the store. A small partitioned room behind the quilted rooms became our kitchen, where our big table and benches took up most of the floor space; a dishpan and red pitcher pump in the backyard replaced Mama's kitchen with running water, and her electric stove was left in the apartment, so the kerosene stove came out again. In the corner of our new kitchen was a tiny room you could hardly turn around in, with a miniature sink and a flush toilet. We took our baths in a washtub, by the table, on the kitchen floor.

We had a cold winter, and our garden was gone until we could plant a winter crop. Daddy was gone most of the time, and we hardly ever saw him or the rents from the apartments. Mama collected five dollars a week from tenants of the rooms, but they often didn't have the rent. The power was always going off because renters used electric heaters to get warm and hot plates to cook on. Mama replaced the fuses and talked to them, but they kept using hot plates and electric heaters, and Mama kept replacing fuses.

Bessie offered Mama one of her washing and ironing jobs, but Mama knew Bessie had a family to feed too and wouldn't accept her offer. She looked for other solutions. Mack rigged a setup to parch peanuts in a barrel that he turned on a spit over a fire to toast. He could tell when they were parched by the way they smelled. We filled little paper sacks with the peanuts and sold them door-to-door.

Mama was expecting again in April, but she packed a lunch on weekends, when we were out of school, and we walked to the middle of colored town early in the mornings and huddled around fires in fifty-five-gallon barrels with bean pickers who waited to go to the fields. Big field trucks with sides and benches in the back would line up in front of the run-down shacks and businesses and lower ramps for the pickers to board. Field bosses stood beside the back of the trucks and tried to convince workers to climb in their truck, saying, "Our vines have the most beans," or "We're paying thirty-five cents today." Mama listened to the chatter to learn who was paying the most per basket, and we'd climb up the ramp of that farmer's truck.

Once we got to the field, we'd put Baby Lulu in a bean box lined with a blanket and move it along with us. We picked beans and sang spirituals with the other pickers. They helped with the kids as we picked our way, in the black muck, down the never-ending rows of beans in the blistering sun. I sometimes thought Mama was at peace and got her spirit renewed singing spirituals in the field.

She loved the tall sunflower plants that towered over the rows of beans, between every-so-many rows, that were meant to protect the bean plants from wind, but there was rarely a breeze. The sunflowers blocked some of the black muck as it swirled into blackouts when the big trucks drove through the field to collect the baskets of beans, and Mama teased that it helped us to blend in with the other pickers. Our fellow pickers thought that was funny. By midmorning the sun came up and warmed the chill, and by midday we were all sweltering in the hot sun. By the end of the day, we'd return home covered with smudges of black muck and sweat and breathe lightly as we rode home betwcen the sweaty pickers.

One afternoon in early April of 1948, Mama crossed the road to move Bessie to another part of the pasture. Just as she pulled the stake out of the ground with Bessie's rope attached, the neighbor's dog came running toward Bessie, barking. Bessie bolted, yanking Mama to the ground where she landed on her stomach. She got things under control and anchored Bessie in a greener part of the pasture and came home, looking dazed, and lay down. She told us she had stumbled moving Bessie but was okay. She told Lois and me to get a dollar from her jar and run to the corner for some Kotex pads. Just as we were going to leave, Daddy almost fell coming in the front door. We knew he was drinking, so we rushed the kids out the back, as Mama was dragging herself out of bed. He was cussing her for being in bed and neglecting the kids. We covered the kids' ears to muffle the profanity and abuse, until we heard a door slam and an engine start. Lois and I hurried inside to find Mama getting back in bed with blood on her nightgown. She looked shaken but was calm as she told us she was all right, then told us to go to the corner for the pads and have Bright Eyes watch the kids. I told Bright Eyes to keep the kids outside while we were gone.

Bo & Jesse, Wine-o shack, Belle Glade

Later, Mama got up to start dinner but lay back down and told Lois and me to go get Dink. We ran across town to Ted's Sweet Shop where Dink was working and told her about Mama bleeding. The shop owner, Mr. Lamb, called the ambulance. He told them to pick Dink up at the shop because there was no house number on our place. Lois and I heard the sirens as we hurried back to find Mama gone.

Dink was by Mama's side in the ambulance as it sped from where we were living, through town, to the Belle Glade General Hospital. The sirens sounded the urgency throughout the little farming town. Mama was rushed through the open doors into the emergency room on a gurney. The doctor on call was contacted at the Belle Glade Golf and Country Club, a few miles away, and informed that she was full term with child and hemorrhaging profusely. He instructed the nurse to pack her with gauze and send her to her own doctor in Pahokee.

The nurses looked sad, as they quickly did as he said, and watched as she was rushed back into the waiting ambulance. Dink prayed as she held Mama's hand inside the ambulance as it raced across the 10.74 miles of winding, bumpy, pine tree–lined roads. Our longtime family doctor, Dr. Spooner, and a covey of nurses waited anxiously as they took Mama into the emergency room of Pahokee General Hospital in our previous hometown.

They worked feverishly over her and wheeled her into the delivery room with Dink clinging to her hand. Her plea to our oldest sister was hardly audible. "Dink…please get along with your daddy… Don't let Welfare take the kids…Keep them together."

Mama's long thick black hair and her petite four-foot-ten-inch form made her look younger than her thirty-eight years. She lay in a puddle of blood after giving birth to a beautiful baby girl, our twelfth sibling, who remained still in her arms, as both floated away into a peaceful hush… A mother's voice—until her last word is spoken—is heard long after it ceases to be audible.

Chapter 11

Grief is the last act we can give of those we loved.
Where there is deep grief, there was great love.
—Annette J. Dunlea, Irish author

The last time we saw Mama was at the First Baptist Church on NW Avenue B in Belle Glade where we had been attending Sunday school. Though neither Mama nor Daddy attended church, Mama made sure we kids were dressed on time to catch the First Baptist Church bus every Sunday morning. It stopped in front of our house where several neighbor kids, Lois, Bright Eyes, Jesse, and I would climb in to go to Sunday school and church.

Both Mama and Daddy were raised in an overly strict evangelical home, and though they both could quote the Bible, neither seemed to still adhere to all the harsh interpretations they were raised to believe. Daddy said, jokingly, if he stepped inside a church, the roof would collapse, and Mama, I believe, was too conflicted with residue from her upbringing to feel comfortable there. The ladies attending this church wore makeup, jewelry, and modern hairdos. Mama grew up being told all these were sins, and though she no longer believed that, she resisted Dink's efforts to talk her into wearing a bit of lipstick; her only jewelry was a wide gold wedding band, and she never had a perm. She said she had attended enough church and tent revivals with Granny to last a lifetime.

At the funeral, Daddy and ten siblings, including me, age eleven, sat in the front pew of the church. Our half siblings, their families, Daddy's brothers, and their families filled a number of rows immediately behind us. A few neighbors, some of Daddy's political friends, and some members of First Baptist Church filled other pews. We were left to wonder why none of Mama's family was there but were in too much of a haze to question it at the time. Dink, nineteen, held our youngest sister, Lulu, who was one and a half, in her lap. Bobby Jean, age three, snuggled close to her. My youngest brothers, Jesse and Bo, ages seven and five, sat tight between our older brothers, Robert and Mack, who remained seated with their heads in their hands. Mack was fifteen and Robert, who fibbed about his age to join the Air Force, was seventeen. He was stationed in Illinois, but the Salvation Army church bought him a bus ticket to come home. Lois, thirteen; Bright Eyes, nine; and I sat between Mack and Daddy. One of our half sisters, Luvera, Verna, or Nellie—I don't remember who—walked in front of us and whispered to Lois, Bright Eyes, and me that we should go up front and tell Mama goodbye.

Beautiful soft sounds of organ music floated from the balcony in the back of the church playing "On the Wings of a Dove," one of Mama's favorite hymns. Daddy stood up and took Bright Eyes's hand and motioned for Lois and me to come. I took her hand, and Lois took mine. We walked up front with Daddy haltingly.

Mama looked like she was sleeping in a bed of shiny white satin. Her long black hair, spread partly on her shoulders and a pillow, contrasted with the whiteness. Our beautiful baby sister was cradled in her left arm, with Mama's right hand resting lovingly on the lace at the bottom of a tiny white baptism gown. Mama's head was tilted slightly down, as if she was humming a lullaby. Our baby sister looked like a doll behind the enclosed glass case of my friend's doll collection. I couldn't bring myself to touch them. I believe I was in shock and incapable of comprehending that this might be the last time I would see Mama.

After the preacher talked about Mama going to heaven, everyone sang, "In the sweet by and by…we shall meet on that beau-ti-ful shore…," but I didn't want to meet in the sweet by and by. I wanted Mama to be with us now.

A lady then sang "In the Garden" and "How Great Thou Art," two songs we often heard Mama sing, as the people stood up and walked past Mama and our baby sister, then in front of the pew where we were sitting. As they passed us, the women, dabbing their eyes, hugged Dink and us kids, and the men shook hands with Daddy and my older brothers. In hushed voices, they offered their sympathies and returned to their pews. As soft organ music continued to fill the room, a man in a black suit closed the lid over Mama and placed a huge spray of beautiful pink roses on the lid. I believe it was our uncles and brother Ithaniel who stepped forward and positioned themselves on each side of the casket. They walked with it, behind the preacher and down the aisle, through open double doors. They carried it down the wide steps and slid it into the back of a long black car parked in front of the church. We were ushered out behind them with Daddy into the back seats of another long black car behind Mama's.

What I remember about the fifty-four-mile trip to Mama's final resting place is the torrential rain as we followed her in the long black car, through the massive, decorative wrought-iron gates of the historic Woodlawn Cemetery in West Palm Beach. We were sheltered by umbrellas as we were led from the car to sit under a canopy, in a row of folding chairs on green artificial turf. Dink directed us to the chairs in the back where we sat with our older brothers. She and Daddy stood behind us. Rain pounded the canvas overhead and formed waterfalls over the sides of the canopy. We listened to its drumbeat as we watched the men in black suits lift Mama's casket from the back of the black car and place it on a stand draped with black velvet. Blasts of wind blew the black velvet skirt open, exposing a cold-looking metal frame. Two men in black unloaded lots of flowers from the long black car and placed them on stands and on the ground around Mama. I remember thinking, *Mama loves these beautiful flowers.*

The minister started to talk but stopped in midsentence. A yellow taxicab approached the canopy from the opposite direction of the narrow path on which we entered, between rows of graves. It pulled up close to the canopy, facing the long black car, and stopped. The doors of the taxi opened, and a black umbrella popped open. We saw Granny step out from the front seat. Mama's sisters, Aunt Evelyn, Aunt Helen, Aunt Bessie, and Aunt Madeline, appeared under umbrellas that opened against the downpour as they stepped out of back seat. Granny ducked under the canopy, closed her umbrella, and came to the back where we were. Not looking at Daddy, she hugged

Dink, Robert, and Mack, then knelt and pulled Lois, our younger siblings, and me to her, as she dabbed her eyes with a handkerchief.

Our aunts insisted on seeing Mama. Without a sound, two men in black stepped forward. One removed the big spray of flowers, and the other slowly opened the lid of the casket, exposing the stillness of Mama and our new baby. Everyone moved back as our aunts stepped closer and dropped their opened umbrellas under the canopy, by the casket. They stood together and sobbed as they stared at Mama, for what seemed like a long time. Granny stayed with us. Our aunts picked up their umbrellas and stumbled out into the rain. They made their way to the back, behind everyone. They clung to each other under two umbrellas, as they sniffled silently, half soaked from the swirling rain that continued to fall.

The minister cleared his throat and continued. The pounding of rain on the canopy finally subsided enough to hear him ask us to sing "Amazing Grace." He ended with a prayer, and those who were standing dispersed, but we remained in our seats. Daddy stepped away from us and stood by his brother, Uncle Vester, allowing our aunts, who pretended not to see him, to visit with us. They told us Uncle Hilas, Mama's brother, was overseas in the Army, or he would have come too. Our aunts and Granny hugged and kissed each of us before climbing back into the taxi that was waiting to take them back to the Greyhound station to return to North Florida. Granny rolled down the window and said, "Call me if you need me." That was the last time we saw or heard from Mama's family until we made contact later years. It's strange. My siblings and I never discussed, during our childhood, why they never contacted us, but discussing it as adults, my sisters and I concluded they knew Daddy well enough to know he would not give up "his young'uns," and being around him, knowing how he abused Mama, was possibly more than they could bear.

We ten siblings returned to Belle Glade in the black car with Daddy. The ride was long, sad, and quiet. We older siblings sniffled and took short breaths, attempting to keep our composure for the sake of our younger siblings. After an uncomfortable ride back to Belle Glade, we parked in front of our apartment house in Belle Glade, where our belongings had been transferred back, from next door. I believe we were all numb. Though Dink and Robert had not spoken to Daddy since he moved us into the abandoned building in the wino camp, they stayed several nights with us before Dink returned to her apartment across town and Robert to Chanute Field in Rantoul, Illinois.

There are no words to describe the dark, heavy fog that hung over our household that I thought would never clear. We all had our individual ways of coping. Uncle John, Daddy's brother, offered Mack a job after school and weekends for ten dollars a week. When Mack wasn't working, he spent hours in the pasture with Bessie, who surely missed Mama too. I would find a place behind the chicken coops or climb up high in the poinsettia tree next door and cry until I could hardly breathe. When the younger kids were out of earshot, and sometimes when they were not, Lois would rant on how much she hated Daddy. She called him every cuss word she could think of. Mama would have washed her mouth out with soap, for sure. Bright Eyes, Jesse, and Bobby Jean walked around in a quiet, sad daze, and Lulu would stand by Mama's feather bed and ask, "Where's Mama?" We were desperately trying to help each other find our way through the fog.

I, who previously loved school, couldn't stand hearing voices of kids laughing and playing on the playground. How could they be laughing? How could they be playing? Why was the radio still playing Mama's songs when she could not sing along? Why were people going to movies and slurping chocolate blizzards? Didn't they know something real bad had happened? Didn't everybody stop everything when the news came over the radio that the Japanese bombed us?

In spite of their efforts not to show it, the tension between Dink and Daddy was felt by all of us. She cooked and talked to Lois, Bright Eyes, and me about being responsible and taking care of our younger siblings and each other. When she realized Daddy was spending all his time with the younger kids and wasn't drinking or going anywhere— except occasionally for a couple of hours at night, when he might have had a drink or two, but was never angry or abusive—she returned to her job and room across town. She kept a close watch on us.

Daddy went quietly about cooking and caring for us and attempted to engage us all in conversation but didn't push the point. He talked to Jesse, Bo, Bobby Jean, and Lulu, who clung to him, and though they seemed confused, they loved being with Daddy—before now, we all did, when he wasn't drinking. I felt guilty, because I knew Daddy, not his usual teasing self, was hurting too, but I was so angry. My love and hate for him were on a collision course. I wanted to forgive him, as I knew Mama would want me to do, and yet, that deep hurt I felt inside screamed revenge. I wanted him to rot in prison, but I knew that wouldn't happen. Sheriff John Kirk, whom Daddy helped get elected, and local lawmen didn't arrest him when we called for help before. Last year, we called the police when Daddy was drunk and beating Mama. They sent a deputy whom Daddy knew. He saw how he had beaten Mama! He told Daddy, "Urbie, as a friend, you need to come with me and sleep it off. You'll be okay in the morning." I don't think he took him to jail—but probably to his home—because, as before, he was out and about the next morning. Whom should we blame…the dog that scared Bessie, Daddy who abused her, the doctor who wouldn't treat her, or the police? Maybe *all* of them!

We lived from day to day, expecting to wake up to find Daddy gone. Dink would come often and cook a special casserole or bring us a surprise. She occasionally brought us seven movie tickets to see a matinee at the movie theater next door to where she worked. After the movie, we would fill almost all the stools at the soda fountain in the sweet shop, where she would spend her week's pay feeding us hamburgers and ice cream. Of course, we never realized until years later that it would come out of her meager weekly check.

Eventually, when the initial shock faded slightly, and we could bring ourselves to talk about Mama, it seemed to help. We attempted to continue our family tradition of singing together after supper for the younger kids' sake. We tried singing silly songs, but we often ended up singing her favorite hymns. The silly songs didn't seem funny anymore. I believe, without knowing it, we were trying hard to override the sadness with happy distractions, as we had observed Mama doing so many times—sing silly songs, play silly games.

Daddy started a winter garden with the youngest siblings, but we older kids resisted anything he suggested. Hoeing and digging kept them busy and created a subject for a conversation during meals. Even if it was only between Daddy and them, it broke our mealtime silence and helped ease the tension. He stayed with us almost 24-7, leaving only for a few hours occasionally at night, and sometimes men he worked with came to the apartment, and they would go outside and talk. He allowed us to grieve, as he silently cooked, put meals on the table, and did everything around the apartment.

After a few weeks, he said he needed to get back to work during the day. We would learn years later that his "work" was being one of the kingpins for illegal gambling in the Glades—bolita, roulette, wagering on wrestling matches and greyhound races, and even rooster fights. *Bolita* means "little ball." It's an early version of lotto that came from Cuba. Little balls with numbers are picked from a round cage for weekly drawings. We didn't realize the beautifully colored banty roosters he kept in wire cages behind our apartments were for cockfighting. There was much we didn't know at that time.

Lois and I took over cooking. Mama had tried to teach us how to cook, but we were not always as attentive as we should have been. We thought we knew more than we did. One night, our whole family sat on the front porch and shelled a basket of black-eyed peas as we had our traditional sing-along. The next morning, Lois and I washed mason jars and proceeded to can them in Mama's pressure cooker, as we had watched her do so many times. We would normally ask Dolly, who lived in one of our apartments, for help. Daddy would sometimes hire her to help us, but we thought we knew what we were doing. We put the shelled peas in the jars, added a teaspoon of salt, covered the peas with water, and tightened the lids. Lois added water around the jars and put the lid on tight. We went outside to play while they cooked. Suddenly, we heard a loud explosion. We ran to the kitchen door to find black-eyed peas on the ceiling, walls, and in every nook and cranny of our little kitchen. There was broken glass everywhere. We were cleaning it up when we heard Daddy's car. I held my breath. When he saw the mess, he said, "Whoa, what happened here?" We told him—without mentioning we went out to play. We thought he'd be upset, but he said, "I'm glad you young'uns didn't get hurt." As he helped us clean up the mess, he said, "We'll just have to get us some more black-eyed peas and have Ms. Dolly show you girls how to use that pressure cooker." Once we learned we were not in trouble, Lois and I laughed, thinking that Mama would have told us to "lick our calf over"—what she always said when we didn't do something right the first time. We found we were often saying what Mama would have said or done; we were slowly healing.

We favored Daddy's way of making us "make up" when we argued or fought. Mama would make us hug and kiss, and she had a switch handy if we didn't, but Daddy bought boxing gloves and made us duke it out in the square boxing ring he roped off in the backyard. I remember our brothers boxing, but Lois remembers us boxing each other too. Daddy never missed an opportunity to have fun while teaching us a lesson about life.

We had so many memories of Mama all around us. When I thought of how happy we were to be back in our apartment with a kitchen sink with running water and a shower at the end of the back porch, I would think of Mama in the wino camp and become very sad that the only inside water in the shack was in the toilet and a miniature lavatory. For baths, we carried water from the pump in the backyard in buckets and heated it on the kerosene stove to fill a washtub on the kitchen floor. Lois, Bright Eyes, and I would bathe the younger kids before we took our turns, according to age. By the time it was my turn, there was a layer of scum floating in the tub from the kids playing in the dirt. Mama would say, "This Belle Glade muck is great for growing potatoes, so make sure you clean their ears so they don't wake up with potatoes sprouting out of them." We would tease the younger ones by checking to see if they had potatoes in their ears. I loved watching the scum swirl down the drain of the shower at the apartments. I reminded myself, "Remember to tease the kids about potatoes behind their ears."

It was easy to fill my mind with the sad things that happened at the wino shack, but I tried hard to think of something good. About the only thing I could conjure up was a happening with the homeless man, Seabo, who often came to the back door of the shack, asking for a drink or something to eat. If we were short on food—like with no seconds—Mama would take a bit from each of our plates to make him a plate. But if Daddy was home, he would do that too, but he would hand him an old two-burner kerosene stove we kept for camping and tell him, "If you trim these wicks, Seabo, I'll feed you." I didn't understand. One day, I asked, "Daddy, why do you make him trim the wicks on that old stove? We don't even use it, and besides, he trimmed them the last time he came."

Daddy said, "Listen, Buzz, if you can help it, you should never take a person's dignity. It hurts a man's pride to have to beg for food, so if he earns it, it's not a handout, and he keeps his dignity."

Things were getting better, because we were beginning to be able to share memories and even laugh about some of them. One such laugh was ignited when we sorted items in the drawers of Mama's sewing machine and remembered a night at the wino house. A month before Mama died, we were all sitting on the floor as she sewed. She had just cut out two little dresses from feed sacks. Flour came in white cloth sacks from which she made our underpants, and chicken feed came in sacks with printed patterns from which she made our outer wear. She would pull a string on emptied sacks, and they opened into squares of fabric. She had been collecting printed ones with little pink and blue flowers for months. She was happy when she got the final one needed to make matching dresses for Bobby Jean and Lulu before the pattern was discontinued.

We finished our baths and emptied the bathwater from a wash-tub on Mama's plants in the back of the wino shack. Sitting around her on the floor, we ran elastic through waists of the underpants she made, as she continued sewing. Lois wanted store-bought under-pants and wouldn't run the elastic through hers. Mama said, "They'll be here when you need them bad enough to finish them." Ignoring Lois's attitude, she continued working her magic with the squares of pink and blue flowers. It seemed that the rhythm of her feet pumping to and fro on the wide foot pedal of her Singer sewing machine—and the needle bobbing in and out, as it zipped along the fabric—was keeping time as we sang. We started singing a silly song we made up: "My daddy Urb had a still round the curb, where he ran off a gallon…" She laughed but made us stop singing that one.

After our black-eyed peas incident, we found three pairs of flour sack underpants and two little dresses in Mama's sewing. They were all finished except elastic in the waist of the underpants and hems and buttons on the dresses. Lois and I hemmed crooked hems and sewed buttons on the two dresses (that would probably fall off), and saying nothing, Lois unpinned the strips of elastic Mama had measured and attached to each pair of underwear, ran elastic through the waists, and tacked the ends together, as she had watched Mama do. I know Mama was watching when Bobby Jean and Lulu's blond curls bounced as they pranced and spun around in their new dresses after we finished them. I know she was looking down, and thinking, *You should have listened...I tried to tell you that someday you would need to know how to sew.*

Bo, Daddy, & Jesse

Daddy & kids

Chapter 12

We must embrace pain and burn it as fuel for our journey.

—Kenji Miyazawa

There were only two months remaining in the school year after Mama's funeral. About two weeks before school let out, Nell Smith with Family Services came by on a day Daddy happened to be home. She saw we were living in a clean home, had food and supervision, but she told him about the County Children's Home in West Palm Beach and suggested he take us there after we finish the school year to be supervised and exposed to a good education. They talked for a long time, and he thanked her for her concern but made it very clear that he could care for and educate his young'uns better than they could. He bought pork chops for supper and normally would show Lois and me how to cook them, but he prepared the meal that night. As we sat around the table, he told us about his conversation with the welfare lady and explained why we could not go wandering around the neighborhood and that we needed to keep the younger kids in the house, or have Lois, Mack, or me always with them.

That frightened me, because our friend Betty Woods, who was Bright Eyes's age and lived with her mama and little redheaded brother in our wino rooms, had just disappeared one day. They moved out of town and left her behind, and an old gentleman, named Pops, who lived in our apartments took her in, but she mostly stayed and ate with us. A neighbor said one of the ladies from welfare was asking about Betty and might have taken her. People from welfare were often in our neighborhood, and I think most of my friends' mamas were more worried about them taking their kids than getting beaten by their drunken husbands. Daddy assured us they would not take us, because he had a plan—we would return to Michigan to pick cherries with the Showalter kids and have a vacation we would never forget. We were all surprised he would give up campaigning for John Kirk and Dewit Upthegrove for the whole summer before the upcoming election.

The next thing we knew, Daddy and Mack were working on our car day and night. They dissected our '36 Chevy coupe behind the cab, added tandem axles and wheels, and built a large wooden enclosure behind the cab with a glass window and a door at the back. We had a motor home for our adventure. He said we should name it, and I cringe, remembering how we painted "Mule Train" on each side. Mule Train was a popular Tennessee Ernie Ford cowboy song that was climbing the charts at the time: "Mule Tra-ain…clip-pity clopping over wind and rain…Get to the top, never stop, never stop…Clip-pity-clopping a-long."

Jesse and Bo became excited when Daddy offered to take us fishing the weekend before school was out. Their excitement made it harder for us older siblings to resist everything he suggested, as we had been doing. Another reason was that not long ago, we camped there with Mama, and we were looking for diversions, not reminders. I thought of that weekend: Daddy was renovating the apartments, and Mama was expecting, but we were all sweltering after setting up our tent. Daddy said, "We should dive in the canal under the trestle and cool off."

Mama said, "Absolutely not, Urbie. There's moccasins and gators in that water!"

He teased, "Those snakes are more afraid of us than we are of them, Shorty, and we could no sooner jump in and they'd be all the way to the Kissimmee River."

Jesse said, "I'll bet if we jump high from the trestle—of course, when the train isn't coming—that would scare them away, for sure."

Mama said, "Urbie, why do you put such crazy ideas in these kids' heads?"

We dug worms from the rich black muck and fished with cane poles Daddy cut from clusters of bamboo growing along the

Dink's day off, Belle
Glade 1948

Dink, 1948

canal bank. Mama cleaned and coated the specks and bream we caught with cornmeal and cooked them and a big pot of grits over our campfire, and we filled our tummies; and after playing hide-and-seek around the banana trees and bamboo, Mama sang with us as we sat around the blazing fire Mack built.

At the time, I wondered how I could I think of that day and not realize they would only remember the fun, so we packed a picnic and went fishing at the trestle. The kids had a fun, memorable day.

We were sad that Dink moved to West Palm Beach, where our sister Verna, her husband, Charlie, and three kids lived. She would bring cake, cobbler, or clothes she made on her days off from Fitz's Drive-In, where she waitressed. Though their communications were strained, Daddy told her, "We'll be leaving before daylight on the last day of school, because if they want to take these young'uns, they'll have to find us."

Mule Train was loaded with our tent, camping supplies, and musical instruments, and Dink took the day off and spent the night so she could see us off. We were awakened before day smelling biscuits, ham, eggs, and grits

Dink cooked for our send-off. Daddy was raring to get on the road, but we were delayed due to fog. Some of the worst auto accidents were caused by hitting a cow in the fog. With open range, you never knew when you'd encounter one in the middle of the road, but we finally pulled out about nine.

Seven of us rode in the back, and we older ones took a turn riding up front with Daddy as his copilot and student of navigation. Mule Train drew a lot of attention. When we were driving through Atlanta, Mule Train stalled, and we all got out, except Lulu and Bobby Jean, and pushed it off the road. Someone with a big camera pulled over and took pictures of us. The episode was terribly embarrassing.

Daddy stopped in visitor centers for information about events and points of interest and asked locals. I don't know in what order, but in our travels that summer, we saw many waterfalls in North Carolina, driving the long way around the mountains because Mule Train wasn't up to climbing over them. We saw reenactments of the Civil War; visited colonial Williamsburg and Jamestown, Virginia; went through some of the Smithsonian museums in Washington, DC; and Daddy wanted us to tour the White House, but they were closed for tours. We toured the Hershey Candy factory, and as we drove through Pittsburgh, Mack remarked that the whole city, covered with soot from coal-burning steel plants, looked like we did when we left the bean fields. Daddy made sure he kept up with state and national elections, buying newspapers along the way, and made occasional telephone calls back to Florida.

En route to our final destination to return to the Hansen's Orchards in Bear Lake, someone told Daddy about a small strawberry farm in southern Michigan requesting pickers for a big order of berries without stems for a local jelly and jam company. The canning plant would pay more per flat because more time was required to pick them without stems. The small job would be good to fill the brief time before the early cherries would be ready in Ohio, so we set up under a big shade tree and went to work.

We were amazed at how much Lois was picking; she was smoking all of us. When the field boss came and told Daddy someone was leaving the stems on and covering them with a top layer of berries without stems, Daddy was very upset and proceeded to find out who the culprit was. We all had that competitive gene, but that's when we learned how very competitive Lois was—and would remain her whole life—and she usually was the best at everything she took on. She got a good chewing out, but to her, the worst punishment was swallowing her pride and apologizing when Daddy took her by the nape of her neck to the field boss.

We moved on to Clyde, Ohio, where we stayed in a migrant camp and picked cherries that ripened earlier than farther north. We set up camp a distance from the rows of attached rooms where the workers from Bradenton, Florida, stayed and the many Mexican families' tents on gravel pads, behind the rooms. Everyone hauled water from a pump.

We worked with the other pickers, climbing up and down ladders and moving them from tree to tree all day, and by the end of the day, we were bone-tired, but we still looked forward to joining everyone around a community fire ring. Everyone meandered to the field in front of the tents after eating supper, at the first sound of our Mexican friends' mariachi instruments and singing. Before we left, we learned Spanish songs, "Cielido Lindo (Ay, Ay, Ay, Ay)" and "El Rancho Grande," and taught them a couple of ours. We also learned a few words of Spanish from kids that Daddy told us not to repeat. These families from Mexico were very hard workers who were warm hearted, were lots of fun, and had a real zeal for life.

I remember how, after a long day in the orchard, Mack, Lois, and I took the younger kids and headed to the high-water tank behind the orchard we had heard about, with soap and towel for baths. After we bathed the younger kids from water dripping from the tank overhead, Mack, Lois, and I climbed metal steps, dropped into the tank of water in our clothes, dog-paddled around, and took our baths while the kids played below. My younger brother Jesse recalls how we wouldn't let them climb the ladder. We enjoyed these baths a couple of times before they came to a screeching halt, after overhearing adults talking back at camp: "Where in the hell was her mama when she drowned? She had no damn business in that tank where we get our drinking water." We were horrified to learn it was our drinking water, but especially about the girl drowning. I don't believe Daddy found out, until we were grown, about our baths; he thought we were taking baths in a shower we rigged by our tent. I knew Mama was watching over us.

We packed up Mule Train and started on our way to join our friends in Bear Lake, Michigan. We had driven over a hundred miles before we realized our three-year-old sister, Lulu, wasn't with us. When we looked through the window into the cab and found she wasn't in the front as we had thought, we pounded on the window until Daddy pulled over. What a scare! Daddy found a telephone booth and called the office of the camp and asked the crew chief to check with the family whose little girl she always played with. After an eternity of waiting, a lady from Immokalee called us back at the pay phone and told us she was safe and sound with her family—that they waited to move on until they heard from us, because they knew Daddy would be back. We were delayed getting to Bear Lake, but we never left any of the kids during our summer travels again. A mandatory head count was put in place, and Lois, Mack, and I were each assigned younger kids for which to be totally responsible for the summer. Mama was still watching.

The Hansens were glad to see us. They had heard about Mama from the Showalters with whom we had kept in touch. We set up our tent in the same choice place and were glad to see the Showalter kids the first day of picking. We left Bear Lake the second year with a forlorn feeling, but we had a lot of fun under our belts: competitions in the orchard between the Showalters and each other; hearing the orchard buzzing with song; daily hikes across the ridge to the lake for baths and corn roasts; a tour of a local cherry-canning plant; and trips into town on Saturday nights for movies, popcorn, ice cream, and a newspaper.

We had had a wonderful summer, and it was time to return home to register for school, and we were anxious to see Dink. Mrs. Hansen made a supply of jam for us from raspberries we picked from her garden. The Showalters came to see us pile into Mule Train and soberly wave goodbye as we pulled away.

That was the last year we went to Bear Lake; however, my husband, Pat, and I returned recently on one of our many RV trips, over sixty years later. We were able to contact three of the Showalters and meet them for breakfast; none of them had ever left the area. Their farmland had been sold, but JoAnne, the oldest, lived in the family home, which was just as we left it. Bonnie Jean, who had a mutual crush on Mack, was now a grandmother. She took the day off from work to give us a nostalgic tour. The Hansens' home looked the same with new paint, but the barn and outbuildings were less sturdy looking. Hansen's Cherry Orchard had been transformed into an upscale horse farm with white fences and a gigantic beautifully landscaped mansion. The ridge we once hiked over to take a freezing bath in Lake Michigan was covered with homes and condos, and the breathtaking field of wildflowers were no more, but Old Facefull was exactly as we left it. Bonnie Jean said it would always be there as a testament for the stories they tell their grandchildren about the wonderful long-ago summers of their childhoods with the Meeks clan. I teased her, "I can just hear you telling your children and grandchildren how, in spite of having to work like slaves to pay for your own school clothes, walk a mile in the snow to take icy baths in the lake, and eat corn to keep from starving, we all made the best of it." We laughed.

She said, "We always felt such a let-down when your dad would say, 'It's getting chilly—time for us Florida Crackers to head south.'"

We were so excited when Daddy said we were going to stop in Indianapolis on the way south to buy school clothes and attend a stockcar race. He parked on a back street, and we wandered around several blocks before we found the JCPenney store. We were a little confused in the store when Daddy asked where the fabric department was, but we followed him into the elevator to the second floor. We were disappointed when he asked the clerk, an older lady, "Could you help my girls here pick out some nice cloth to make some school clothes?" It went over like a brick.

Lois and I protested, almost in unison, "Daddy, we don't know how to sew." To which he replied, "You need to learn. I'll get someone to teach you."

When we wouldn't participate in choosing fabric, he started picking out the most atrocious-looking designs, so we stepped up to the plate and grudgingly picked some out. We left disappointed with some underwear and socks for all of us and pants and T-shirts for the boys.

We arrived home earlier than originally planned. Before we left for Michigan, he hired Dolly Taylor, and her husband, Jake, who lived in one of our apartments, to care for the apartments and our cow, Bessie, while we were gone. He hoped Dolly could help with the kids and be our "go to" person in-between Dink's visits on her days off from West Palm Beach.

We went back to school, and Daddy went back to his work and campaigning for Kirk and Upthegrove. He rode a beat-up old bicycle that someone gave Mack all over Belle Glade and into the migratory camps, registering new voters and revving up those who were registered.

I was in sixth grade, and Lois was in the eighth. She joined the band, choir, and everything she could to fill all the hours she could. She was seldom home after she became a majorette with the school band. She entered the spelling bee and placed in the top five winners in the county for her age group. Bright Eyes and I joined Girl Scouts, and I started taking acrobatics, tap, and toe-dancing lessons from Gladys Chester, who came once a week from West Palm Beach to teach in Belle Glade. Another girl and I led the band onto the field doing acrobatics at a couple of the Belle Glade Rams' football games. Mack joined FFA (Future Farmers of America), and Bessie won a blue ribbon at the county fair. He also placed high in the county spelling bee for his age group, but he soon quit school to work full-time with Uncle John. When I wore a skirt I made to school, a couple of girls giggled, pointed at me, and said, "Did your little brother make your skirt?"

I told Daddy, "I told you they would make fun of it."

He said, "They're more to be pitied than shamed, Buzz. Maybe they were just jealous, because they don't know how to sew." He asked Dolly to help us with sewing but told her to make us do it all ourselves with her help. I had good incentive to make a better skirt—

and I did, and so did Lois, though she got a needle through her finger before mastering pedaling the sewing machine and guiding fabric at the same time. Daddy made the pedal higher with boards so we could reach it more easily.

Eventually, Lois, Evelyn, and I all became skilled at sewing, making drapes, and upholstering as we grew up.

Though we had great support at school from teachers, band and choir directors, and most of the kids, sometimes, we were not always as well accepted by some of our classmates. In a small town like Belle Glade, being from a family where your daddy was known as a gambler who drank and beat your mama, and whatever else they knew, preceded you. Once, when I was in third grade, I dropped my pencil and the boy behind me leaned over and picked it up, and someone said, "Don't touch that. It's got Meeks on it," and he dropped it. Mrs. Granger, my third-grade teacher, walked over with a piece of paper and asked me to take it to the office. After I came back, both boys apologized to me, and everyone was nice to me after that, but we were learning to hold our heads up and work through it, remembering, "They're more to be pitied…"

Uncle Fletcher and Aunt Lu moved to the outskirts of town, and I was glad we saw Naomi and Hazel, my favorite cousins, at school. Hazel was my age, and Naomi, Mack's. I was saddened when I saw Hazel in gym class. Unfortunately, things were not as politically correct back then, and the school would not excuse a student from gym class for religious purposes. Hazel dressed out for gym wearing her brother's long pants under a long-sleeve, high-neck dress, and the kids would point and snicker. I felt bad I complained about wearing my silly skirt. I believe my skirt bothered me more than her unusual gym clothes bothered Hazel. She, Naomi, and Aunt Lu were beautiful, loving, and uncomplaining souls.

Between work and campaigning, Daddy attended almost all our activities and offered suggestions on our performances. He told Lois, "You can't be shy. You have to strut like you're leading the band." As he gathered the tails of his coat together in front of him, he stood erect, threw his head back, and strutted to show her. We all laughed, but he had a point. He pretty much told me the same thing: "To dance with confidence and passion." He took us to the circus when it came to town and to a carnival in an open field, where he stood and watched while we rode all the rides and tossed rings at stuffed animals or nickels in carnival wear dishes, hoping we could take home a prize, like Mama's valued bowl and vase Mack took home to her from previous carnivals.

Daddy was elated November 2, when Kirk and Upthegrove were reelected with the support of the black vote. Daddy was presented with a shiny red men's bicycle with a basket and horn, and John Kirk hired Wilbur Burney, believed to be Palm Beach County's first black deputy and one of the first in Florida. An article in the *Palm Beach Post* regarding an interview with Wilbur two years before he died at eighty, in 1983, said that when Kirk sent his chief deputy to get him, he was leery and recalled he asked, "Just in black town?"

When the deputy showed him a badge and responded, "That's what you're going to be. You arrest anyone who breaks the law, black or white."

He said that was what he wanted to hear and was sworn in right there, and that afternoon, he marched in a parade in uniform. He said he met with some resentment but that Kirk later sent him throughout the state to recruit blacks. He went on to form the Association of Negro Deputy Sheriffs in 1952, when Florida had three black deputies who were banned from the Association for Deputies. After his death, retired DeSoto County Sheriff's deputy George Brown, of Arcadia, took the article to his sheriff. Brown had been sworn in three years before Burney. DeSoto County passed a resolution to recognize Brown during their centennial.

Race relations were slowly starting to improve as Florida moved into the second half of the twentieth century but had a long way to go.

Daddy, being a "yellow dog Democrat" (he'd rather vote for a yellow dog than a Republican), was elated the Dems swept the elections. They won the presidency, the House, and the Senate. Truman beat Republican New York governor Dewey, who was so strongly expected to win that the front page of a right-leaning Chicago newspaper, the morning after election, mistakenly read, "DEWEY

DEFEATS TRUMAN," which was retracted in smaller print the next day.

Later that November, Uncle John, my favorite uncle, invited us eight kids and Daddy for Thanksgiving dinner without first clearing it with Aunt V. Daddy lectured us about minding our manners. Lois and I should help Aunt V, and Mack should keep the kids playing outside until dinner. When we arrived, though Frances, who was my age, tried to make us feel welcome, Bonnie, Lois's age, stayed in her room, and Aunt V stayed in the kitchen and left the welcoming up to Uncle John.

After being told she didn't need any help, we took the kids outside until dinner was ready, but I was beginning to feel uncomfortable, like she was upset. I had a knot in my stomach and could hardly eat. After dinner, Aunt V had Bonnie and Frances clear the table, do the dishes, and wouldn't let us help. I wanted to believe I was being overly sensitive but couldn't shake the feeling that we were not welcome there. Really, why would she be upset that she suddenly had nine more people to accommodate on Thanksgiving?

The worst Thanksgiving of my life taught me a life lesson: I vowed to make an effort to assure anyone whoever came to my home that they were welcome.

Chapter 13

Grief is a nasty game of feeling the weakest you have ever felt and morphing it into the strongest person you will have to become.

—Windgate Lane

One Saturday, we all piled into Mule Train for a visit with our half sister Verna, in West Palm Beach. We wanted to visit Dink but didn't think we should ask, since she and Daddy were still not talking. We asked Daddy if we could go to the casino swimming pool across from the beach, by the pier in Lake Worth, where Verna took us once when we came to her house with Mama. Verna told him it was safe with two lifeguards and offered to keep the younger kids so we could enjoy time with her older kids, Sonny, Brealie, and Gabby. He said, "Okay, pile into Mule Train, and I'll take you." We spent over half the day at the pool and we weren't supposed to leave the pool, but Sonny and Brealie wanted to show us the tunnel that went under the road to the beach, so we went exploring. We played in the ocean and got stung by jellyfish and had a hard time concealing the welts, and after a half day in the sun, we were so sunburned we could hardly move. In spite of that, we had the time of our lives and I thought we just had to convince Daddy to move to West Palm Beach, to be closer to Dink and the beach. I think Mama would love the beach too.

We talked about West Palm Beach around Daddy every chance we got. He loved his friends, gambling, and political life on "The Muck," as he referred to his beloved Glades, but he told us he was trying to work something out with Uncle Fletcher so we could move. When he acquired the apartments from Uncle Fletcher, they were almost in unlivable condition, and Daddy, with our help, refurbished them. Uncle Fletcher was a preacher with no handyman talent and no desire to do anything but preach. After Daddy learned construction was booming in West Palm Beach, he made what he called a win-win deal, on a handshake, with Uncle Fletcher. I heard the deal went something like this: Uncle Fletcher's family would live rent-free in exchange for collecting and sending the rents from the other apartments to Daddy so he could rent in West Palm Beach and pay the mortgage payments on the apartments.

Daddy got a job as a carpenter with Kendall Construction, building FHA homes in West Palm Beach, and Mack got a job with Hawthorne Roofing Company to help with expenses. We moved to West Gate, a little neighborhood nestled on the outskirts of downtown where Dink and our half sister Verna and her family lived. We rented a little green house on Genesee Avenue with plenty of sleeping areas—two bedrooms, a sunporch/hall with a bed, and a murphy bed in the wall of the living room—an eat-in kitchen with a gas stove we were afraid to use, and a bathroom with our first ever bathtub. The big yard had grass; an orange, a mango, and a banana tree; and a chain-link fence, allowing the younger kids to run like free-range chickens without one of us with them every minute.

Daddy bought us a wringer washing machine, and Mack strung clothes lines across the backyard. When Dink warned us about avoiding getting our fingers caught in the wringer, I told her about the time Mama got her hair caught in the wringer of that old short-lived washing machine Daddy brought home. "Lois, Bright Eyes, and I were playing by the chicken coop, near Mama's washing machine, when Mama yelled. We looked up and saw her leaning over the washer, and her long hair was caught in the wringer, but her tummy was too big for her to easily reach the button to shut it off. By the time we ran over to help, she had managed to reach the shut-off button." We were afraid to use the washer, as well as the stove.

It seemed that everything we did reminded us of Mama—using the same pots, pans, and dishes she used; listening to a song on the radio; and even popping the clothes in the air before hanging them to get the wrinkles out so they would be easier to fold when they dried—but at least we were beginning to be able to talk about her more and no longer had the daily reminder of the wino shack. We were beyond happy to be out of Belle Glade.

West Gate was a small community of less than a square mile with modest houses, and most owners were too poor to worry about paint or landscaping, but there were a couple of teachers and small-business owners with nice homes there. With women starting to work outside the home and the economy beginning to revive after the war, many families living in public housing now had two incomes and could afford to buy a home in West Gate. The charm and beauty of the small community was its people and the beautiful, sprawling poinsettia trees that delightfully distracted a stranger's eye from the many run-down bungalows on tiny plots of land. Many dwellings were dwarfed by humongous old trees that had long ago outgrown their allotted space and expanded their loaded branches over the narrow dirt roads.

In season, orange, mango, guava, and avocado trees offered free healthy after-school roadside treats. The high-reaching limbs of *Ficus* trees were great for dreaming or building a sky-high hideout with borrowed scrap lumber from neighbor's construction projects.

You had to earn your stripes in our new neighborhood. Newcomers had to prove themselves, but having family there already—our sister's kids, who were the ages of me, Bright Eyes, and Jesse—got us automatic approval. Most families were large like ours, and mamas who didn't work looked after the kids of those who did. Though most kids were told not to leave their houses while parents worked, most of us did—the boys would gather at the "Boys' Club," high in the bow of a tree behind Sonny's house, play marbles, root the peg, jump board, or wander around the neighborhood looking for mischief. We girls gathered at each other's houses to play jacks, jump rope, jump board, or hop scotch and practice doing cheers or make fudge and divinity from sugar, cocoa, and ingredients skimped from different kitchens. We would all rush home in time to scuff through chores before our parents got home. Lois, Bright Eyes, and I giggled, remembering how we hid dirty dishes in the oven and burned pots in the backyard so they wouldn't smell. We pulled out our instruments before Daddy got home as if we'd been practicing.

We did lots of things we knew Mama wouldn't like and felt ashamed when we would think of it. She definitely would have made us "lick our calves over."

Mack bought an old car that got him to work every day, but also, unexpectedly, it helped get him accepted in West Gate. Working on his car in the front yard attracted other teenage guys like orange blossoms attracted bees. He soon had a flock of friends, including Clyde Lewis, Ronnie Zill, and Maynard Wright. After work and on weekends, if they were not in Mack's car at the sand pits skinny dipping or horsing around playing jokes on each other, you'd find them working on Mack's jalopy at our house or Clyde's. One day Mack and Ronnie came home with a cardboard box that was taped closed. Mack called Dink from the kitchen door, "Dink, come here, I brought you something."

She said, "I can't come now, Mack, I'm cooking." He brought it inside, handed it to her, and said, "Open it."

The kids were all saying, "What is it? What is it?" So she brought it into the living room so they could see. When she felt something shift inside it, she dropped the box, and a scared black snake slithered across the floor and quickly disappeared under the Murphy bed, causing a panic. Leaving dinner cooking on the stove, Dink screamed and ran out the door and wouldn't go back in, and the kids scattered in all directions screaming. Mack and Ronnie were laughing at first but got real serious as they opened the bed and chased the snake all around the house until they finally corralled it and directed it out the door. None of us seem to remember what happened to dinner, but I'm sure Mack didn't eat dinner at home that night. He never would have tried that on Mama. She would beat him half to death with her egg spatula, and I don't believe she was looking down laughing. She was extremely afraid of snakes and had taught us to think of all snakes as being deadly.

Daddy was working all the overtime he could get and insisted I continue dancing lessons with Gladys Chester, and he took Lois, Bright Eyes, and me to Leggett's Music Store to buy instruments of our choice to learn to play. I got a Gibson guitar, Bright Eyes chose an accordion, and Lois got a steel guitar. We started taking music and singing lessons from Katy Coffey.

Every Friday night, Daddy would load all of us and any kids who wanted to come along in the back of the truck, and we'd go downtown to the talent show. Three winners were chosen each week by applause and would compete for a grand prize at the end of the month, somewhat like *America's Got Talent*. With our entourage, we often won.

Lois, Bright Eyes, and I sang and played our instruments as the Meeks Sisters' Trio, singing such harmony songs as "Blue Moon," "South of the Border," "Red Sails in the Sunset," "We Ain't Got a Barrel of Money," etc., and silly ones, such as "Slap'er Down Agin Pa."

Our trio and another friend from West Gate, Patsy Merchant, were two of three winners who sang on a local radio show and advanced to be on the *Arthur Godfrey Show* in Miami. And once, after Lois dropped out to pursue other interests, Bright Eyes and I, then a duet, won the honor of being guests of Charleston Heston and his wife for dinner and his performance in *Mister Roberts* at the Poinsettia Playhouse in Palm Beach. We were nervous, but they were so nice and we enjoyed their company, and being the first time we had seen a live play, we loved seeing him act, but the theme of the story was out of our interest range at that time.

Our younger siblings were so cute—and good—they performed, singing "Five Foot Two," "The Chattanooga Shoe Shine Boy," and other cute songs, as they danced and made jivey gestures. As they grew older, Jesse dropped out to hang with Mack and learn about engines with a dream of racing at the Palm Beach Speedway, and Bo could be found fishing under the Southern Boulevard Bridge anytime he was out of school—and all too often, when he should have been in school. Mama would have been so happy that we were all singing, doing the thing she loved so much.

We became a part of the West Gate family, and Daddy, the pied piper of West Gate, always had fun projects going in our backyard with lots of help from the neighborhood kids, like building a doghouse for our dog or making a workable bike out of two old ones he picked up that someone threw out.

If there was a good movie playing at one of the three drive-ins in town, we'd pass the word, and half of West Gate would be at our house and pile into the back of Mule Train just before dark. Daddy would drive us to the movie. He'd park way in the back so it wouldn't block the view of others and hook the speaker from its cradle on the rearview mirror, because Mule Train had no doors. Some of the kids would scramble out of the truck and rush to the seats that were set up in front of the concession stand, hoping they would not all be taken. Others would climb on the hood or on top of Mule Train with their pillows and blankets to watch the movie. Daddy would take his folding chair and newspaper to the concession stand and find a light to sit under to read until the movie was over. We made our own popcorn and fudge at home, so the theater never made any money from us, but we sure got some good memories from them. We would drop everyone off at their houses after the movie.

There was a little neighborhood pub around the corner from our house. The owners were the Cusworths, a Catholic family with a lot of kids. They lived in a fenced house behind the pub that was set way back from the road and away from the pub. You could not see the house from the road. The Cusworth kids went to a Catholic school in town and were not allowed outside their yard to comingle in the neighborhood, but the neighborhood kids were invited to come to them. Behind the pub were eight wooden benches built close to the ground facing a big freestanding white wooden structure used as a screen to show cowboy movies and cartoons every Saturday night, if it didn't rain.

Neighbors would gather at the pub with their kids, and after everyone had whatever Mrs. Cusworth had cooked up for family night—a free bowl of chili or stew or a hot dog—parents would usher the kids out the back door for the movies, while they paid for a mug or two to chug as they talked about weather and the politics of the day. Daddy would make us sing a few songs before the movies, which at first was embarrassing, but we were glad he was proud of us, and everybody loved it and would suggest songs for us to sing or learn.

We never really got to know the Cusworth children well. They were rather quiet and shy, and it bothers me that I can't remember any of their names, but I well remember the kindness of their family.

Dink was still working at Fitz's at night and got a second job, checking groceries at Lovett's grocery downtown, that later became Winn Dixie. She spent all the time she could with us, helping with cooking and cleaning, kept the kids a supply of play shorts with elastic waists, and tried to make sure we had a decent wardrobe. She sewed Lois, Bright Eyes, and me matching short gowns to wear in the talent contest and made all the costumes for my dance recitals.

One day she came over on her day off. She was dead tired, but she cleaned the house and put a pot roast in the oven, then showered and put her hair up in curlers. She had a date that night. She lay down for a nap but couldn't sleep on curlers, so she turned on her tummy with head extended over the end of the bed. We always curled our hair with strips of rags and had never used real curlers. When Lois came home from school, she was fascinated with the idea of Dink's curlers. She took them out of her hair and curled her hair with them. When Dink woke up, Lois had curls and she had damp straight hair. Lois said, "I didn't know you had a date. Clyde is coming over to help Mack work on his car tonight, and I wanted to look good." Dink was furious but, as usual, gave Lois a pass. Mama would be proud of Dink's patience with Lois.

*****

Daddy was not one to say anything derogatory against family, regardless of what they did, but we were beginning to hear an occasional belittling of Uncle Fletcher. He told Mack, "When a man can't keep his word, what the hell is he doing preaching the Word of God?" Apparently, Uncle Fletcher was not making payments as agreed. I think the fact that he didn't keep his word bothered Daddy more than being short of money. Somehow, we managed, but we could see Daddy was concerned about keeping us busy, now that school was out. He told Mack the only way he could figure it out was to take a break from lessons and travel all summer, so he'd know where we were and what we were doing until school started again.

When Mack told the boys about our summer plans, I don't think they thought it out of line to ask if they could go along. They said they could pitch in to buy his gas, if Mack could drive Jenny, and they could follow us in Mule Train. When Mack asked Daddy, he said, "That's fine if they pay their own way and understand that it's a lot of hard work." I could tell Mack was very excited, and I was happy for him.

Before we left, we had another passenger, an old gentleman Daddy picked up from somewhere, who had followed the crops most of his life and was dying to go one more round. His name was Pop Perry. He was thin, rather stooped, and like Daddy, chewed tobacco, which we hated. He had no living family, and Daddy kind of adopted him.

When Jenny and Mule Train were loaded, and we were leaving for our adventure, half of West Gate was there to bid us farewell. Verna and the kids were there, along with Dink, who had filled a box with peanut butter and grape jelly sandwiches, bananas from our banana tree, and carrot sticks. There was a certain sense of security knowing we would be returning to our little green house and our West Gate family in time for school.

Chapter 14

*When angry, count to four. When very angry,
swear.*

—Mark Twain

Mama would love that Mack was now driving and had his own car and three new friends, but she would not be happy that he was talking

GUESTS ENTERTAIN ON 'YOUTH ROUNDUP'

PEAKS' RADIO PROGRAM IN WIOD STUDIO

The royal welcome mat was spread in WIOD for these youth from West Palm Beach, creating goodwill between the youth from South Florida. All were winners of a talent contest in their home town. On the left are the pretty Meeks Sisters, Lois, Evelyn and Betty Sue, who sing in harmony. On the right is pert Patty Merchant singing, "Buttons And Bows." Three other winners appeared on television on the Cracker Jim program.

Meeks sisters' trio

about joining the Army when we returned from our adventure. That's probably why Daddy agreed to allow his friends to join us for the summer. I know she was looking down, smiling, seeing Mack and his friends teasing each other as they drove north, following Mule Train.

We puttered along, stopping quite often to put water in both radiators from roadside canals, but finally reached our first stop to pick strawberries in Battle Creek, Michigan. Daddy had what he called a crew meeting, setting down guidelines for the trip. Of course, Mack's friends would keep the money they earned, but they had to follow our family's rules: everyone would work every day unless they were sick, everyone would get up early and go to the field or orchard together, and everyone would be respectful of plants, people, and each other.

Mack's guys were excited as they pitched the big tent they'd brought together a short distance from ours, outside the cluster of trees behind us. Across the field were a couple dozen tents belonging to Hispanic pickers from Plant City, Florida. Among them were several pretty girls that Mack and his guys had an eye on, and a couple of nice-looking teenage boys who started flirting with Lois the first day of work.

After work that day, Lois and I were getting things set up in our outside kitchen to cook supper, when Clyde approached in a huff. He grabbed Lois's shoulder and angrily spun her around and said, "I saw you flirting with those guys today."

When she pushed his hand off her shoulder and started to say something, he slapped her across the face. I was shocked, because Lois told me they were going steady, and I thought that meant they really liked each other. Without thinking, I walloped him across the head with the iron skillet I was holding and ran for my life. Spotting Daddy talking to some men across the field, I flew toward him with Clyde right behind me. I dove and locked my arms around Daddy's legs, almost knocking him down. Daddy held his hand out to stop Clyde and said, "Hey, what's going on here?"

Rubbing his head, Clyde proceeded to tell him how I hit him with a skillet, and I told Daddy the reason I did was because he slapped Lois. Daddy always told us, if we didn't jump in and help our siblings if they were in trouble, we'd be in trouble when we got home.

He said, "A skillet isn't all you'll get hit with if you ever touch one of these young'uns again." I was glad Daddy didn't ask for more details, because before we left home, Lois made me promise I would not tell Daddy that she and Clyde liked each other, or he wouldn't let him go with us.

I was surprised Daddy didn't send him back south, but Clyde got the message. It was a little awkward for a few days, and though I knew he wouldn't do anything after the encounter with Daddy, I still steered clear of him for a while.

Clyde continued to try to talk to Lois and asked Mack to talk to her, but once you split your britches with her, it takes a long time to mend those britches—like the rest of the summer for Clyde.

The guys were gung-ho the first couple days, and they soon realized picking strawberries wasn't as much fun as working on Jenny. We all had a *breaking in curve*—for our backs, that is—except Pop Perry, who just worked slow and steady, without complaining. He seemed happy as he darted in and out of his little pup tent, cooking his food on a little fire, enjoying being back in his element.

After the strawberry harvest, Daddy heard there was a call for workers to harvest potatoes and cucumbers in Terre Haute, Indiana. As always, Daddy checked the truck over before heading to a new location. He and his mechanic crew installed a new coil and flywheel on Mule Train, changed a tire, and checked the spare on Jenny in preparation for the long trip.

The last few things were loaded into the truck. Mack boosted the younger kids in the back of Mule Train, and Lois and I climbed in behind them. Mack got in his old Plymouth where the guys were waiting to see what was next, as Daddy counted heads—a habit he started last summer, after we left Lulu in Ohio. He patted the hood as he slid in next to Jesse, his copilot, and said, "We're off like a herd of turtles," as we pulled away.

Before we got into Indiana, the engine started running hot. We had to keep pulling over and stopping for the truck to cool off. Daddy would scoop up water in his stained felt hat from the irrigation ditches along the highway to pour into the steaming radiator. Like an old movie reel in slow motion that keeps breaking, we would stop and go, limping past endless fields of potatoes and cucumbers planted in red clay, ready to be picked. And never having picked potatoes and cucumbers before, I thought, *I'd much rather be picking cherries off a ladder than working on my knees in that red clay.*

We finally arrived at the farm of our new employer, two days before we were to start work, and found the office in the company commissary. After Daddy checked in and got information he needed, we drove down a narrow road to the area designated for tents and trailers of the farmworkers. Many migrant workers already had their tents and some trailers set up on raised gravel-filled forms. We drove past barefoot children playing in the dirt road at the entrance to the camp. Many rows of tents, within four feet of each other, lined each side of the road and cul-de-sac. The children stopped playing and moved out of the road, as they snickered and pointed to Mule Train. We smiled and waved as we drove past them. They teasingly pushed each other toward our truck as they laughed and waved back. We thought it would be fun to have so many new friends, but Daddy tipped his hat to a group of men in work clothes, standing under a tree, talking, as we circled the cul-de-sac at the end of the dirt road, and drove out the exit gate. I don't think he liked the tents packed in like sardines; he liked open spaces.

We rode around dirt roads in the backwoods for what seemed like hours, seeing only miles of open fields of crops and an occasional farmhouse and barn with scant signs of life. Daddy would slow the truck every so often and look around. Suddenly, he pulled the truck to the side of the road. The engine idled as he rested his foot on the brake and looked across an open field overgrown with weeds, at a small shack by a huge tree in the distance. He slowly steered the truck over clumps of weeds toward the big tree. He stopped the truck close to the porch of a dilapidated, weathered, and deserted shack with a partly caved-in and rusted tin roof. The panes of glass were missing from the windows, and boards that once covered them dangled at awkward angles. The leafy branches of the huge tree that stood beside it extended over most of the shack, shading it from Indiana's harsh summer sun.

Daddy stepped out and to the front of Mule Train, as he removed his hat and stood there, looking all around. Swooping the air with his dirty old hat, he said, "I knew we'd find a good place. Look here, this is a piece of history! This was a sharecropper's home," and he proceeded to tell us the history of how his family was sharecroppers in Alabama, when he was growing up, before Grandpa bought his farm in North Florida. "Now, y'all get out and check out this big walnut tree while Mack and I look inside. Get the hammer out of the toolbox and crack open some of them." He had his arm over Mack's shoulder as they came out. "Just look at this! Look what we found! We'll cover the roof with our tent and fix this place up to stay in. There's plenty room in the shade of this tree behind the place for you boys to pitch your tent."

They stretched our tent over the roof and secured it with rope tied to stakes driven in the ground. Mack, Clyde, Ronnie, and Maynard set up their tent under the shade of the tree beside the shack. Daddy found some loose boards to create our kitchen. He built a long counter, about eighteen inches wide and low enough for us to reach, along the wall by the kitchen door. We set up the kerosene stove with the iron skillet, other cooking utensils, and the few dishes, cups, and eating utensils we had not broken or lost on one end of the shelf and saved the other end for the kids' table for meals. We had cardboard boxes from the grocery store in town to give each of us as our own drawer to organize and store our clothes, just as Mama had done at the cane field and on our first trip to Michigan. We were pleased with our setup and settled in to an agreed routine of sorts. Lois, fifteen at the time, and I, thirteen, would take turns cooking and switch off a week at a time taking care of the younger siblings, with the help of Bright Eyes, who was eleven. Daddy was a good cook, but we did all the cooking. He asked, "If I do the cooking, how will you girls ever learn?" Lois and I were becoming pretty good cooks, but when he bought something we didn't know how to cook, he would sit on the kids' low table in the kitchen and instruct us. The weather was warm, but after supper, Mack built a big fire, and we sang along with the uke, harmonica, and spoons while roasting marshmallows and taking turns telling tall tales into the night.

Lois and I fixed a big bag of peanut butter and grape jelly sandwiches, and Mack filled the five-gallon thermal container with water, leaving room to add ice. He sat in the driver's seat with Daddy, as the guys and the rest of us climbed into Mule Train and headed to the commissary. Mack took a bucket inside and came out with a ten-pound block of ice, which he chipped and dumped into the water jug, then he secured to the running board, before slipping back under the wheel. He steered the truck into the line of vehicles loaded with other workers and followed them to a field of potatoes for our first day of work.

The big machine, now upturning rows in the field across the dirt road, had already scooped clumps of potatoes from the earth and dropped them into piles along endless rows in front of us. We each carried a bucket to fill with potatoes to be dumped into the big heavy boxes along the rows for pickup. We were taught not to complain, but Daddy allowed us some leeway to voice our dislike for harvesting potatoes! At lunch, when we complained about broken backs, Daddy said, "I ordered new ones for all of us from Sears and Sawbucks, and they're on back-order but should be in the mail any day now."

He worked right along beside us and allowed us to take as many breaks as we wanted, but having such competitive blood, we took as few as possible so we could brag about how many boxes we filled. For days, rows of workers, including Clyde, Ronnie, and Maynard, who had adjusted to being a migrant worker, stooped and crawled along the mile-long rows in the red clay and sweltering sun, filling boxes, until that field lay barren and ready to till for the next planting.

Daddy decided we needed a break, so we took a day off to tour a nearby potato chip plant to see the results of our hard work. Inspired, Lois and I started competing to make the thinnest potato chips. Our big iron skillet was full of hot grease and thin sliced potatoes a lot of the time. We cooked and ate potatoes every way imaginable—fried, mashed, boiled, baked over campfire, mixed with tomatoes, onions, beans, and whatever we could come up with—and found our favorite was our thin chips piled high between slices of bread with gobs of mayonnaise.

When the first field was harvested, we learned we would switch over to a field of cucumbers the next day. Lois and I were especially glad, because our fingers were sore and were beginning to crack from the dirt and potatoes. We later learned we both had an allergy to potatoes that lingered into our adulthood. For years, our hands would break out when we peeled or handled raw potatoes. Looking back, I wonder if we created that allergy out of disdain.

We learned the first day we picked cucumbers, they don't come off the vine with smooth skins like the ones we get from the grocery or produce stand. They are covered with prickles that are harder on the hands than the potatoes. When Lois and I showed Daddy our hands that still had cracks from the potatoes and had become worse, he filled a pan with cool water, washed our hands gently, and patted them dry. He then smeared lard on them and wrapped them in strips of soft cloth from a white T-shirt. He cooked dinner that night and said we'd go into town tomorrow and get some medicine for our hands and let them heal. Mack and the boys wanted to keep working to earn more money, so they stayed and worked the next day while we went into town to a drugstore on the corner of Main Street. He told Lois and me to show the pharmacist our hands, then bought the salve he suggested and some white cotton gloves. After having ice-cream cones, he took us to see *Annie Get Your Gun* with Betty Hutton. He patiently sat outside the theater door and read the newspaper and waited for us to watch the movie through two showings.

We were all tired as we piled into Mule Train to return home from the movie. I was riding up front with Daddy. Suddenly, I froze in my seat—I got a whiff of a familiar smell. A chilling realization hit me with a flood of memories—Daddy was drunk. He was driving as if he was in a souped-up Ford running from the Feds. Mule Train swayed as it swerved around the winding dirt roads in the pitch-black night. I was nervous but afraid to say anything, knowing he'd been drinking. It was hard to tell the edge of the road from the irrigation ditch. I put both feet on the dashboard to brace myself and prayed as we approached a sharp turn. Flying around the curve, the front tire on the passenger side dug into the soft ground, tossing me into the ditch as Mule Train flipped over and pinned me to the ground. It knocked the breath out of me, but I could hear the kids screaming and scrambling out of the back. I almost blacked out with fear.

The next thing I knew, Daddy was standing over me in the ditch. He gripped the top edge of the truck's door opening that had me pinned, and with a loud grunt, he hefted the truck off me and back on its wheels. I somehow knew then, and have never doubted, that Mama was still watching over us. Mama, with God, must have helped him, because there was no way his slight-built, hundred-and-forty-five-pound body could have lifted that heavy truck by himself! Daddy checked everyone for injuries and was relieved that other than being frightened and having a few bruises, no one was seriously hurt. We reluctantly climbed back into Mule Train, and from the looks on Lois's and Bright Eyes's faces, one word to describe what we were afraid to voice was *fear*—fear Daddy demons had returned. Daddy—cold sober by now—drove back to our place at a snail's pace, then sat in the truck a while before coming inside the old sharecropper's shack we had claimed for potato season. I thought of Mama and wondered what would happen next.

The next day, the guys went to the fields again, but we didn't. We toured the local pickle plant where we saw how pickles were made. Daddy seemed to think this would make us appreciate picking cucumbers, but it didn't. We watched them being washed in big machines, moved along conveyor belts, and dumped into huge sunken round vats of brine with thick, slime-looking scum that formed on top during the pickling process. Another machine filled sparkling glass jars with processed pickles and clear vinegar, before they swirled into a machine that clamped on lids and slapped a colorful label around each jar. It was fascinating to see, but it spoiled my appetite for pickles.

On the way home, Daddy told us he had a new plan and we should get the laundry all caught up and start getting things together. The guys were back from the field when we got home. Daddy dropped us off to cook dinner and do the laundry and asked Mack if he wanted to go with him to talk to a guy at the commissary. "He knows every farm and orchard from Homestead, Florida, to Benton Harbor, Michigan. We need to find something besides these potatoes and cucumbers." Mack jumped in with him, and they drove across the well-worn path to get some information.

It was my turn to cook, but Lois decided we should have one more "potato chip–making challenge" before emptying our grease and leaving the potato fields behind. After stacking a big mound of chips we had made at the end of the shelf for the kids to snack on, we declared we were both pros and called it a tie. I moved the twelve-inch iron skillet of hot grease to the end of the shelf by the door to cool and make room on the counter to make supper, and Lois started gathering laundry just as we heard the truck engine shut off. Daddy and Mack were talking as they walked across the porch to the kitchen door. As Daddy followed Mack in the door, he was saying, "I think that farm in Georgia—" As he let go of the doorknob and started to sit, I screamed, "Daddy, don't!" trying to warn him. But it was too late! He plopped down on the shelf, right into the hot grease in the black skillet. My heart went to my throat and I couldn't make a sound, but the kids' screams mingled with the full power of Daddy's extensive vocabulary of profanity.

Daddy's burns were bad, and Mack insisted on taking him to a doctor, or at least to the medic at the commissary, but he wouldn't go. He sent Mack to get baking soda, molasses, gauze, and tape and made a paste like Mama made for Bright Eyes's arm. He had Mack help him plaster it on his burns and cover it and told us to finish packing to leave the next morning.

It was a long, slow trip home. Mack, Clyde, and Ronnie took turns driving Mule Train and Jenny south, and Daddy lay in the back of Mule Train on his tummy. Maynard didn't have his driver's license yet, but he could change a tire in a New York minute and was assigned that job. We made frequent stops to put water in the radiator of Mule Train, to make a few mechanical tweaks, and for Maynard to change two flat tires. We stopped along the side of the road and spread a quilt on the ground for Lois and me to make sandwiches for everyone. When we stopped to fill up with gas and stretch our legs, Daddy would go into restrooms at filling stations to doctor his burns. After five days on the road, we were all exhausted when Mule Train and Jenny finally pulled into the front yard on Genesee Drive.

I don't remember the name of the town or farm in Indiana, which we voted, unanimously, to be our least loved summer place, but I well remember the terrible incident that caused us to return home to Florida early that year.

Abandoned shack

Chapter 15

No matter how you feel, get up, dress up, show up, and never give up.

—Author unknown

We were very busy getting the kids and ourselves ready to start the new school year. Mack drove Daddy to the job site each morning where he went back to building houses, and Mack resumed working on roofs and would pick Daddy up at the end of their day. We continued to try to get Daddy to go to a doctor, but he would say, "Ain't no sissies in this house. I'm tough," then he would plaster more of his concoction on his bum and keep going. We had been home almost a month, and Daddy was still limping around and wincing when he sat. He mostly stood at the kitchen counter to eat and would say, "I don't have time to sit. I gotta get to work!" Thinking back, I wonder if he kept a *half pint of pain killer* in his back pocket, or stashed somewhere, because I don't know how he did it!

Dink was still coming on her days off from Winn Dixie to clean what we didn't clean, mend our clothes, sew on missing buttons, and often cook dinner for us and leave before Daddy got home to get ready for her waitress job. Though she and Daddy were still not on real good terms, the excruciating pain of Mama's death and the fog seemed to be dissipating slightly for all of us. We were beginning to find solace, rather than feeling sad, when we heard or sang her songs, discussed how she would do things, or shared stories about her. I think Dink was beginning to soften with Daddy too, because she would sometimes cook turnips with ham hocks and make fluffy biscuits and some of his other favorite dishes.

Daddy was always creating competitions between us, and one he initiated when we first moved to Genesee Avenue was a biscuit-making contest between Lois and me. He must have been missing Mama's biscuits. He said, "I got a dollar for the one who learns to make the best biscuits by the end of the month." The race was on! Lois didn't like to cook, but she made a lot of biscuits, trying to win that dollar. Daddy didn't know how to make biscuits, but he'd say, "Ummm, better, but maybe you need a little more baking powder or lard and etc.," but he never commented when we served Dink's, because he knew who made them. We didn't think to ask Dink to teach us until after the contest. Lois won, but even hers were a far cry from Mama's or Dink's.

Mack didn't have to sign up to join the Army. Right after his eighteenth birthday in mid-December, he hit the lottery—of the draft, that is—and his draft papers arrived in the mail. He went to Miami for his physical and was waiting for his final orders. He had been saving money for several years to bring another dream to fruition, one that kept him on the fence about joining the Army. He couldn't be in the Army and ride his very own Harley. Daddy tried to talk him into buying a newer car rather than a bike, but he wanted that Harley and bought it right after we returned from Indiana. I felt bad that he would have to leave his Harley, but I felt worse that he would be leaving us.

We knew Daddy was getting better when he sat down with us for breakfast one Saturday morning and announced, "We're going to have us fun adventure today. Enough of this, letting life pass us by!" He had us help him load a big sheet of corrugated tin, Uncle Vester's old ten-foot flat-bottom boat, a couple of CBS blocks, some chopped wood, and oars into the back of Mule Train, then told me to get the bucket and gloves from the shed. He told Lois to make a big jug of Kool-Aid and get cups and the hot sauce to bring along. Jesse and Bo were really excited, thinking we were going fishing, and Bobby Jean and Lulu were just happy to be going anywhere. Lois did as Daddy told her, but she made it known she didn't want to go. I think she wanted to stay home because she and Clyde were patching things up, and she thought he might come over later to see Mack.

As we were loading up, he told us we were going to have an oyster roast for dinner. Mama loved the water and oysters, and the first, and last, time we went oystering, she was with us. She brought peanut butter and jelly sandwiches in case the kids didn't like oysters, but they all did. He stopped at Winn Dixie and had me run in to get a big box of soda crackers before driving north on US Highway One to the Jupiter Inlet and parking by the old bridge. We dragged the boat out of the truck and down to the water's edge. Daddy stacked the wood on the beach and started a fire with the help of the wind. He had us help him place the sheet of tin over the fire on the CBS blocks. As he walked toward the boat, he said, "Buzz, you keep an eye on Lulu and Bobby Jean, and, Bright Eyes, you watch Jesse and Bo. You know they don't know how to swim, so don't take your eyes off them. Lois, let's you and me put gloves on, take the boat out to those beds, and get us some oysters for dinner."

Lois said, "Daddy, I don't want to pick up those dirty, ugly-look-ing things, and I can't eat them! I'd rather watch the kids."

I said, "I'll go in the boat," and took the gloves from her.

Daddy said, "Okay then, Ms. Nasty-Nice [a name she acquired last summer when she refused to drink from the same water dipper as Pop Perry], you watch the kids. Buzz, bring the bucket and get in the boat." I climbed in the boat, and he pushed off, climbed in, rowed out, and anchored at the edge of a massive bed of oysters. We broke clusters of oysters loose, filled the bucket, and piled them high in the middle of the boat. The fire was roaring when we got back to shore, and we spread oysters over the hot tin. Daddy explained, "They'll let go of their tight grip when they feel the heat—makes them easier to open—same thing with conk shells." To demonstrate, he slid his knife between the slight crack between the two shells, pried it open, and tossed the top shell on a nearby mound of oyster shells from oth-ers' feasts. He scraped the blade under the oyster in the shell, shook hot sauce onto it, and slid it onto a soda cracker. He tilted his head back, put the whole cracker in his mouth, saying "Um-m-m!" as he chewed, and smacked his lips after he swallowed it. Lois refused to eat them at first, but we ate them as fast as he could shuck them, and she, too, ate her share before we left to go home. Bo and Jesse didn't seem disappointed that they didn't get to fish, because they had a great time playing in the edge of the water and sand with Bobby Jean and Lulu.

The next day, we caught the bus to West End Baptist Church with the kids, and Clyde, Ronnie, and Maynard were there with Mack when we got home. Clyde asked Lois to go to a dance that was being held for local teens at the community center. She danced around and was on cloud nine. She made us swear we would not tell Daddy. She told Clyde, "I'll have to meet you there because Daddy will never let me go with a boy." Daddy didn't know she had a date—or maybe he did, because when she asked him about going, he said, "You can go to the dance, but you have to all stay together." She told him it was only for teenagers, but he said if we couldn't all go, we'd all stay home or go to the drive-in movie together.

The dance was held at the West Gate Community Hall. The small one-room wooden building on stilts had steps leading up to double doors that opened to welcome all in the little community for a variety of activities. It was actually the Salvation Army's church building, but Catholic Mass was offered by a visiting priest between the Salvation Army's services each Sunday. It seemed to have one community service or another going 24-7. Meals were served seven days a week for those who were hungry, and blankets and army cots awaited the homeless or anyone who needed a place to sleep on real cold nights. The back area served as a day care for working mothers with children too young for school and was a fun dance hall or venue for events for the community's youth.

We were excited about the dance planned by the local women's circle for West Gate teens. They even arranged for live music by musicians from the Musicians' Union who volunteered for the occasion. It would be a dressy occasion. The night of the dance finally came, and we all dressed in our best with Dink's help. She had somehow gotten Lois a beautiful dusty-blue semiformal dress with two layers of net on the skirt. She looked beautiful. Dink said, "Lois is the oldest, and you will all have your turn getting a fancy dress when you're her age."

Daddy dropped us all off at the dance and waited to see if they let us in before driving off. I think all the teens in West Gate were already there, and we were not the only younger siblings who had tagged along. Lois quickly disappeared in the crowd. Bright Eyes and I took the younger ones to the side of the room where little sandwiches, brownies, cookies, and a big bowl of pink punch with floating oranges and cherries sat on tables draped with white tablecloths. I watched Lois walk outside with Clyde Lewis and another boy and girl and didn't see her again until time for Daddy to pick us up. She suddenly appeared and joined us by the steps where we were to wait for Daddy's truck. We realized Daddy was parked across the road and maybe had been there for a while. I sensed he was angry when he got out of the truck and trudged toward us. He grabbed Lois by the arm and said, "Get in the truck!" My heart sank! I told Bright Eyes to get the kids in the back of the truck as I quickly jumped in the front to be in the middle to separate him from Lois. I don't remember everything he said, but the way he jerked the stick shift into drive and scratched off told us he was plenty angry. The smell of his breath told us he had been drinking, and I was beyond scared. He angrily asked Lois, "Didn't I see you get out of a car, and didn't I tell you to stay with the kids?"

She said, "No, sir. I didn't leave the dance. I was there all night with the kids." One thing we all knew about Daddy, for as long as we could remember, you may get by with murder if you handle it right, but don't *ever lie* to him! I prayed he didn't know she left, but Lois and I both knew he did! He said what we all had heard many times growing up, "I hate a thief and a liar—and you're a liar!" We had not actually seen Daddy drink since Mama died, but we who were old enough to remember knew when he was drinking. I felt like I would throw up right there. My heart went to my toes. He was cursing Lois and swung his fist at her, but I dodged away from him and caught his fist in my left eye. It made him angrier when he missed his mark. The brakes screeched as he pulled into the front yard and slammed his foot on the brake, almost running into the wall. He jumped out and ran to the other side of the truck, before Lois could get out, and yanked her out. Holding her with one hand, he whipped his belt off and told her to lean over the saw horse that was sitting in the yard where he had earlier been cutting boards to build us a picnic table. She jerked loose from him and dashed out of the yard, down the dirt road. He jumped back in the truck and flew around the corner from Genesee Drive down the road in pursuit of her but never found her. By the time he returned, after driving all over West Gate, looking for her, he had calmed down, but we were all in the back bedroom with the door closed. He went into the bedroom he shared with Mack and didn't come out until the next morning when he got up and made us breakfast.

Lois later told me, "I dived into that muddy ditch in front of the Connells' house and waited until Daddy's truck was far up West Gate Avenue. I heard Bunny's big old dog that I hated started to bark. I've never been so scared in all my life. He barked once, then stopped barking, and something very strange happened. Old Tom stopped barking and came into the ditch with me and stayed right by my side the whole time I lay there. After I saw Daddy's truck drive back by and turn into our road, I scuttled down West Gate Avenue towards Dink's apartment, and he stayed right by my side. I have to think that Mama was watching over me. I called Dink at work and told her what happened. She left work and found me with Old Tom just before I reached her apartment. I went to the house the next day while Daddy was at work and took all my stuff and moved in with Dink."

Daddy was upset with Dink for what he called "aiding and abetting." Old memories resurfaced of him kicking Robert and slamming him with a barrel stave when he thought he was lying, and Robert left for the service without resolution. She knew what Daddy was capable of when he was drinking and upset. She knew she had to put some distance between them. Rents were much more expensive in town, but she'd have to find some way to move away from West Gate. Concerned about Daddy finding Lois, she asked Lois to stay the next few days at her friend's house, who lived downtown near Palm Beach High School where they both attended tenth grade. Dink went to her job at Winn Dixie on Garden Avenue nearby. As soon as she finished her shift, she walked to the phone booth at the corner, clutching the classified ads she tore from the newspaper during coffee break. The dimes from her pocket clinked down the slot of the pay phone, one at a time, as she called the numbers she had circled for one-bedroom apartments. As she dialed 2354 for the one downtown on Evernia, she held her breath, *Please, God, let this one be affordable.* She waited for a voice on the other end of the line and slouched her shoulders and leaned against the steel shelf in the corner of the booth, when she got the answer. *Even with my second job waitressing at Fitz's Drive-In, forty dollars a month is still too much.* She knew she would need to buy groceries for two, buy Lois's supplies for school, and pay utilities. She took a deep breath, folded the ad and stuffed it in her purse, and left the booth, walking fast to the corner of South Olive to catch the five o'clock bus home. She said she thought of Mama and refused to feel discouraged.

As she stepped off the bus on West Gate Avenue and Tallahassee, still thinking of Mama, she spotted Mack's old car in front of her little cottage. He too was concerned and wanted to talk to her about Lois being in an undisclosed place. I guess we were all paranoid about Daddy drinking again and a replay of the past. "Look, Dink, Mr. Will's son wants to buy my Harley, and that will give us enough for you and Lois to get into an apartment downtown, and six or eight months' rent. Lois can get a job for the summer."

"No," she said. "You are *not* selling your bike! You've dreamed of having a Harley for as long as I can remember!"

He laughed. "I hate to admit it, but it kinda scares me. I think I bit off more than I can chew. I'm strong for a little guy, but I can hardly hold it up. I should have listened to Daddy on this one, and I hate to admit it to Daddy, but I won't want the bike when I'm on leave, and heck, I may just stay in the Army."

He sold his Harley and rented an apartment downtown for Dink and Lois from which she could walk to Winn Dixie and Lois could walk to school—no more catching two buses between jobs and home and back. Lois agreed to get a summer job when she finished tenth grade, but Dink had a real challenge trying to supervise Lois with her newfound freedom, and unfortunately, most of her new friends were free to do as they wished. Though Dink said she couldn't go out on school nights, she was at the roller-skating rink with her friends almost every night and at the beach every weekend.

Daddy made some weak efforts to act jovial, but we knew he was feeling bad about what happened. Occasionally, he would ask us if we had seen Lois, and before we could answer, he'd say, "Well, she seems to know it all, so I reckin she'll do okay." We made sure the house was clean and dinner was cooked when Daddy got home from work. We held our breath, waiting for another storm, but none came. He was still driving our friends and us to the talent shows and movies on Friday nights, to square dances at Wellman's on Saturday nights, and wherever we wanted to go. Bright Eyes and I continued singing at various functions, but now as a duet rather than the Meeks Trio. Jesse and Bo didn't want to dance and sing anymore—they were more interested in fishing—so Bobby Jean and Lulu became a duet also. The four of us continued taking music and singing lessons. Bobby Jean and Evelyn were both learning accordion, Lulu had taken over Lois's steel guitar, and I was learning the guitar. We really missed Lois but didn't see her very often. I especially regretted that we never got the chance to continue our biscuit challenge.

Mack got his final orders just before Christmas to report to Fort Bragg, North Carolina, for boot camp. He bought all of us gifts—a new electric iron and an ironing board so we didn't have to iron on the kitchen table, dolls for Bobby Jean and Lulu, and fishing poles for Jesse and Bo. He signed up for Daddy to receive his military benefits and paid a number of months' rent in advance for Dink's apartment. Clyde, Ronnie, and Maynard all joined us at the Greyhound Bus Terminal to see Mack off. We were sad but tried to make jokes during the drive there and inside the bus terminal as we waited with him until he boarded the bus. Daddy didn't say much, but when a voice over the loudspeaker announced the arrival of the bus to Jacksonville, he gripped Mack's hand and shoulder. "Mack, this may not be what you expect, and if it isn't, make the best of it. When I went to Atlanta, I sure didn't want to be there. There were some tough times in there, but when I went in, I had only completed third grade, and when I came out of prison, I had more than a high school education. If you look at it right, there's a lot of opportunity you won't have around here. Try to take advantage of it, son!"

Mack nodded his head slightly, as if in agreement. "Yes, sir." We all cried when he stepped into the open doors of the bus.

Dink teaches gut bucket

Chapter 16

We are not meant to resolve all contradictions,
but to live with them and rise above them.
—William Blake

After Mack left, Daddy started driving himself to work earlier because he'd been made supervisor for a big housing project. He was a stickler for being on time and having things organized by the time the other carpenters arrived. He threw himself into his work and was proud that his project was ahead of schedule, but he didn't seem to have the energy for weekend adventures. He would take us to the drive-in movie if we asked, but since he started going to bed earlier, we seldom asked. We were still going to the talent shows and to family night around the corner at Cusworth's Pub, but not much else.

Summer was around the corner, and Robert had moved in with us with his wife, Betty, and Daddy had not mentioned going north.

One night when we were at Cusworth's, a neighbor who was a member of the Moose Club got into a long conversation with Daddy about the Loyal Order of the Moose. Daddy ended up joining the Moose. He attended meetings and occasionally went to the lodge to chat with members about politics and the weather. One night at supper, he told us the real reason he joined the Moose Club was, *in case anything should happen that he couldn't take care of us, we would have a safe and good place to live.* He said they ran a great place for children called Mooseheart; he didn't tell us it was an orphanage. An alarm bell went off in my head. Was he sick or thinking of leaving us? He said it was nothing like that, but it was always good to have a backup plan—to always be prepared like a good Boy Scout. He told us we would visit this place out when school got out and repeated what he

132

had heard: "It's sponsored by the Loyal Order of the Moose, which includes over a million Moose Clubs in the USA and Canada, with members like President Roosevelt. It's located in a place they call Child City on 1,023 beautiful acres in Peoria, Illinois, and has many nice homes with six to twelve kids in each. There're great education programs where every kid is taught a vocation of their choice—mechanics, musical careers, nursing, and about anything you'd want to be. The kids there can go to college without paying, and most of them do go to college, and they start their education at age three. I just want to have the peace of mind that you young'uns will have every chance possible, and in case I can't give it to you, as a member of the Moose, they can. Now, you don't need to worry about this. I plan to see every one of you young'uns all grown up. When you buy insurance, it's not because you're about to die. It's just that—insurance!"

When we told Dink about what Daddy told us, she looked concerned and asked us if Daddy was working or if he seemed sick. We said he was going to work early every day and going to bed early because he was working hard, but we didn't think he was sick.

What happened the next month made us wonder, though. He left for work early as usual, and we walked Lulu to the day care at Salvation Army on our way to school. About midmorning I was called to the principal's office at West Gate Middle School, where I was in seventh grade, and told Good Samaritan Hospital was trying to get in touch with me. The mere mention of a hospital left me numb. My mind went blank, remembering when Mama went to the hospital. They said Daddy asked them to call the school and let me know he had a little problem but was now okay and would be home tomorrow morning. I wasn't fully convinced but felt a little better.

I left school immediately and, with legs that wanted to collapse, ran to Verna's house to tell her. I guess he didn't want to call Dink, and maybe they didn't know how to get in touch with Verna. She told me to bring the kids to her house after school, and in the meantime, she'd find out everything to let us know. I called Dink at work and told her. Verna took us all up to see him that night, and Dink was there with Lois, but Dink stayed outside because she was afraid it would upset him to see her. They wouldn't let any of us kids in, but Verna saw him and gave us the report. He'd had a heart attack but was now okay, and she said he was in good hands. They wouldn't release him the next day, but he got dressed anyway and called Verna to come get him. When we saw him after school, it was an effort for him to get in and out of a chair, his breathing seemed labored, and he looked white in the face. We knew he wasn't okay—he couldn't fake it that time.

Nell Smith, head of Palm Beach County Children's Services, was constantly attempting to convince Daddy that we would all be better off if he would agree to put us in the County Children's Home. He wouldn't consider it before, but after his heart attack, he was forced to do so. Though the county home was not his choice, he talked to us, telling us we didn't have to make any immediate decision, but asked if we would want to tour the home to meet the children there and Mother Pace, who ran the home. Reluctantly, we agreed to tour it. Daddy arranged it and assured us we were not going to be forced to go if we didn't want to, that we'd figure it out like we always had before.

As we drove into the circular drive in front of the big wide steps up to the double wide doors of the entrance, we noticed many children of all ages peeping out the windows of the dormitory wings attached to each side of the big reception room and office. A little lady who was quite old, wearing thick low-heel white tie shoes from the forties, and her gray hair back in a knot, stood at the top of the steps with a welcoming smile. She shook hands with Daddy and greeted him as if she had met him before—and I am sure she had. "Hello, Mr. Meeks. I'm so glad you all came. Mrs. Smith told me all about you and your family."

Daddy introduced us, placing his hand on our heads, "This here is Buzz, Bright Eyes, Jesse, Bo, Bobby Jean, and Lulu." Mother Pace swallowed and raised her eyes and tilted her chin as she heard our names, but smiled and shook each of our hands.

She said, "You can call me Mother Pace. That's what the children here call me."

As we entered the reception room, they let us take our time inspecting everything while they chatted. Most of the wall space of the spacious room was covered with framed pictures of the children who lived, or had lived, in the home in various groups: the Boy Scout troop; girls taking cooking lessons; the elementary kids' classes who attended classes on the grounds; and individual boys from the home circled in group pictures of football, basketball, and baseball teams from Northboro Junior High and Palm Beach High Schools. But the one picture that took my breath was in an arrangement of individual children. There was my friend Betty Woods, who disappeared from Belle Glade! I interrupted Daddy's conversation and, pointing to Betty's picture, asked, "Is Betty here?"

Mother Pace said, "Oh, my dear, Betty was adopted by a local policeman and his wife after she joined us several years ago." I wanted to ask more about her but didn't. I quickly said, "Daddy said, if we came here, it would only be for a short time, and *we* could *not* be adopted."

"Yes, that is correct. We have many children here who will only stay until their family situation gets straightened out, and that would certainly be your case." I felt a sense of relief.

Two older kids who lived there, Mary Anne and Frank, appeared to give us a tour. We were shown a room across from the office with shelves loaded with clothes and shoes of various sizes that were donated for the children's wardrobes. Down the halls were identical layouts: on each side, before entering the girls' dormitory to the left and boys' to the right. We passed a heavy door, which had a small window with bars, that Frank said was "the pokey" for bad kids. The walls on both sides of the dorms each had ten or twelve beds with white bedspreads and a small trunk at the foot of each bed. Each dorm had shower and toilet stalls and wall-hung lavatories. Cheerful yellow curtains framed the many windows above the beds. We met some of the kids who were meandering around in the dorms and on the playground, who were very friendly. Our younger siblings were happy, mingling with them on the playground equipment, oblivious to the fear and apprehension Bright Eyes and I were feeling. We immediately liked the cooks, Maybell and Ethel, who called all the kids by nicknames, which made us feel at home. Mary Anne said they didn't use nicknames when Mother Pace was around. We were cautious of the two matrons we met who would oversee Bo and Jesse in the cottages Bo and Jesse would be staying in. They looked stern and not very cheerful. We were very happy to learn that musicians came to the big room every Wednesday night, and Frank informed us that Mary Anne had a beautiful voice and sang on those nights, at weddings, and outside occasions. They told us they hoped they would see us again. We told them, "You probably will."

In the meantime, Verna got in touch with Uncle Vester. He was living on his cattle ranch on the outskirts of Belle Glade, near the abandoned migrant housing we had lived in with Mama after we lost our home in Pahokee. He came to see Daddy in West Palm and suggested we go live with him. A five-star alarm went off in my head—I did *not* want to move back to Belle Glade but knew we couldn't abandon Daddy, and there was the problem of no one to watch Lulu while we were in school while Daddy was sick. We knew Dink would know what Mama would want us to do, so Bright Eyes and I discussed it with her and came to a difficult decision: the younger four kids would go to the home, and Bright Eyes and I would stay with Daddy at Uncle Vester's. After Daddy got well enough to take care of himself, Evelyn and I would join the kids in the home where we would all stay until Daddy was well and back to work.

When we told Daddy our plan, he said, "I want you all to stay together. Your mama would want that, and I will be just fine with Vester and back on track at the yank of a cat's tail."

Using a favorite expression of his, I said, "Daddy, we've already made an *executive decision*, and that's that." He smiled and shook his head. He knew, as well as we did, that he would be alone at the ranch most of the time while Uncle Vester took care of his store in town and other business.

I tried to placate myself, thinking, *It may be fun with a horse, cows, and goats on Uncle Vester's ranch*, but I couldn't convince myself. And besides, remembering how Bright Eyes backed into a big cactus when an old dog with no teeth barked at her and how she was scared of the horses at Hansen's Orchards, I knew she would hate it.

The kids seemed okay when we explained about how Daddy needed us, and the fun they would have with all the kids while we were gone, but we miscalculated their reactions. I'll never forget driving away from the children's home, leaving them on the front steps. Jesse was clutching Lulu, who was hysterical, kicking and scratching, trying to follow us, and Bo had his arm around Bobby Jean, who was crying. They had become very attached to Daddy, but Lulu to the extreme. She was okay when we were all together, but she didn't let Daddy out of her sight when he came home after work and on weekends. It was excruciating to remember. Just three years before, she was walking around the wino shack, asking, "Where's Mama?" But we knew we had to take care of Daddy for now.

Daddy's eyes were reddened as he turned to us and said, "You need to stay with the kids," but we both shook our heads and choked out a guttural *no* as we held back tears and fought to keep our composure. I motioned with my hand for him to keep going.

I was sick to my stomach thinking about walking down the same dirt road to catch the same school bus to go to the same school as when we lived near the ranch with Mama in the deserted migrant housing, but the decision was the right one. Mama did many things she didn't want to do and we could too. Trying to ease my mind, I said, "Bright Eyes, I know Mama will be looking over the kids while we're gone." She nodded in agreement.

Palm Beach Co. Children's Home

Children's Home Scout Troop

Chapter 17

*Twenty years from now you will be more dis-
appointed by the things you didn't do than by the
things you did, so throw off the towlines, and sail
away from the safe harbor.*

*Catch the trade winds in your sails. Explore.
Dream. Discover.*

—Mark Twain

Mrs. Nell Smith talked to Daddy about recovering in the Palm
Beach County Nursing Home, which was on the same property as
the County Children's Home, but Daddy said he had Bright Eyes
and me, better nurses than they had there, to take care of him. We
knew, given a choice, he would not go to a hospital or nursing home.
We had everything packed to go to Uncle Vester's ranch in Belle
Glade, which wasn't much because our house was furnished when
we rented it. Daddy arranged to return to disassemble and move his
magic machine from the backyard later.

Daddy, Bright Eyes, and I went to the Children's Home to
see the kids before we left for Belle Glade. As we entered the big
room where the kids were called to meet us, they all came running
to Daddy. Bobby Jean was crying, and we couldn't understand what
they were saying about Lulu, who wasn't there. The blood drained
from Daddy's face, and my heart stopped when we got them calmed
down enough for Jesse to tell us, "Daddy, Lulu screamed and cried,
but Mother Pace gave her to a lady and man who took her with
them."

Daddy darted into Mother Pace's office where she was talking
on the phone, "What the hell is going on here? Where's Lulu?"

She quickly hung up the phone and closed the door as she tried to explain, "Now, Mr. Meeks, I'm sure Mrs. Smith explained that we don't have babysitting facilities here for children who are four and a half years old. We hold them here until we find a good foster family, and Shirley is with a very nice family in Lake Worth."

Shirley? Did she mean Lulu? I couldn't remember the last time I heard Lulu's given name. She had never been called anything but Lulu. I barely remembered that *was* her given name. Daddy blew up. "What the hell are you talking about? The idea of bringing my young'uns here was to keep them all together!"

"Now, Mr. Meeks, she will have the best of care, and you can pick up the others on visitor's day, the first Sunday of each month, and take them to visit her."

Daddy wasted no time getting to Mrs. Smith's office in the county courthouse. Bright Eyes and I sat on a bench outside while he talked to her. He wasn't happy when he came out. He was short-winded, and we were afraid he was going to have another heart attack as we followed him over to Commissioner Lake Lytal's office in the same building. He had campaigned to get Lake Lytal elected. He looked exhausted but a little relieved when he came out and said, "We're working things out about Lulu." Commissioner Lake Lytal was very involved with the children's home. He visited and ate dinner in the dining room with Mother Pace, the matrons, the nurses, and children on the first Sunday of every month.

Bright Eyes and I went to Uncle Vester's to take care of Daddy, leaving the younger kids behind. His ranch was on the outskirts of Belle Glade, near where we lived previously. We walked that dreaded dirt road to catch that dreaded bus to school, but Daddy wasn't resting as the doctor ordered. He was back in West Palm Beach almost every day, working on the situation with Lulu.

The first visitors' day—only two weeks after the kids were put in the home—Daddy, Bright Eyes, and I picked up Jesse, Bo, and Bobby Jean from the home in Mule Train and bombarded the little house where Lulu was living. I don't remember the young foster parents' names; they were very nice but seemed overwhelmed at our invasion. When they mentioned wanting to adopt *Shirley* and saw our reaction, they quickly dropped the subject. We were always so glad to see Lulu, and her us, but it was excruciating to leave with her in hysterics and her foster parents unable to calm her down.

When we picked up the kids to visit Lulu the next visitors' Sunday, it was strange to hear them referring to each other by names they hardly knew. Until the kids started school, some of us were called nicknames at home by our relatives and friends and didn't even know our given names. Some of the names Mother Pace insisted they use were not even correct—Lulu would be called her real name, Shirley; Jesse his real name, Jesse; and Bo, his real name, Marion; but Bobby Jean's real name *is* Bobby Jean, and Mother Pace insisted she would be called Barbara! Mother Pace apparently didn't like nicknames or Southern culture. She completely confused them with her corrections. When they mentioned "Mama," she would say, "That would be your *mother*." When they referred to what they had for dinner, she would say, "That was your *lunch*—dinner is at night." We didn't like it, but Daddy told us to do as she said.

When Lulu became hysterical again at the end of our second visit, her foster mother still couldn't calm her as we left. They decided Mrs. Smith would have to find another foster family for Shirley, because they wanted to adopt, and they knew that wasn't going to happen with her. I don't know what made Mrs. Smith think Daddy would ever allow her to be adopted. The kids had only been in the home five weeks when Lulu was returned to await new foster parents. I believe Daddy was drawing his strength to get in and out of bed from frustration. He beseeched Judge Robbins, the county juvenile judge; Mrs. Nell Smith, chief counselor of county juvenile court; and Lake Lytal, county commissioner, to help him keep the young'uns together, *like their Mama wanted*, until he could get on his feet enough to take us out. They made the exception. Shirley stayed, and Daddy insisted the kids needed us more than he did, so Bright Eyes and I gladly left Belle Glade and joined them in the home.

Bright Eyes became Evelyn (her real name was *Dorothy Evelyn Loraine*), and I, Buzz, became Betty Sue. Whether we liked it or not, we had to call each other Shirley, Barbara, Jesse, Marion, Evelyn, and

Betty Sue around Mother Pace; but we did as Maybelle did when we were out of her earshot.

Evelyn registered in seventh grade and I in eighth at Northboro Junior High, where Jesse and Bo attended elementary on the same grounds. The younger kids and those in the home as delinquents were schooled on the premises. The children's home was not only an orphanage and a temporary home for children with family situations; it also housed the county's juvenile delinquents with minor infractions. There were some pretty rough-acting kids there, but the majority was well behaved and very nice. Sometimes you had to keep an eye on your belongings, and a few of the kids were anxious to pick fights or run away and got locked in the pokey. When I told Daddy, he said, "Like Father Flanagan at his home for boys said, 'There's nothing the matter with boys that love, proper training, and guidance will not remedy.' This is a good place for them."

Bobby Jean, Lulu, Bright Eyes, and I were together in the girls' dormitory. Though Mrs. Sanford was the matron for our dorm, Bright Eyes and I were two of the oldest girls, and it seemed natural to take charge of the younger ones. We taught them how to curl their hair with rags or newspaper, permed their hair, and created little shows to be performed on Wednesday nights when the musicians came. Mother Pace allowed me to bring Mama's sewing machine to the dorm to make outfits for our shows, family duet performances, and talent shows that Daddy was allowed to take us to. It felt strange to have meals prepared and laundry done for us, to have so much time to do other things. The older girls and boys were allowed together to set the tables, place food on them, serve milk from a big machine in the kitchen, and wash dishes in huge sinks under the surveillance of Maybelle, the head cook.

Being the youngest in the Home, Lulu became the princess of the whole place. Mother Pace's son, Uncle Hal, and his wife, Aunt Millie, often ate meals with Mother Pace at the home, and their daughter, Jenny, who was Lulu's age, often spent the night. Lulu would stay with Jenny in Mother Pace's apartment and sometimes go home with her. Lulu got lots of special attention, and no one would dare pick on her or Jenny, or they would have to deal with Mother Pace. Bobby Jean didn't make friends as easily as some kids. It concerned me that she was used to having Lulu to herself and might have felt left out at times. In the beginning, Lulu and Bobby Jean would still cry when Daddy drove away after a visit, but we were usually able to console them.

Bo and Jesse stayed in one of the cottages close to the main building with Mrs. Edwards—a very old lady who had little tolerance for boys and ordered timeouts at the drop of a hat. At ages eight and ten, they joined the cub scout troop at the home and soon made friends.

Dink came on the occasional Wednesday nights when guests were allowed to join the kids for the musicians and came to most of our school activities. Dink could get Lois to come along occasionally, but Lois was either in school, working at Murphy's Root Beer Stand, on a date, or doing the thing she loved most—skating—so we didn't see her as often as we liked.

By the time Daddy became well enough to return to work, school was out for the summer. The company he worked for rehired him as a carpenter to work on a project down the street from the children's home, so he moved back to West Palm Beach and rented a room downtown. Mule Train had finally bit the dust, so a trip north was out, but Daddy was not up to that yet, anyway. He could hardly pay rent, let alone pay someone to watch us. We were a little conflicted. We wanted to be at home with him, but there were many things going on with the kids in the children's home—the Elks Club, Shriners Club, Women's Club, and about any club you can name, sponsored activities and outings for children in the home. Evelyn and I went to summer camp, where Monte Markham, who later became a well-known actor and director, was a counselor. We took swimming lessons; went bowling and skating; attended baseball games, plays, and even an opera, which was a big mistake! We almost got kicked out of the theater because as hard as we tried, we couldn't stop the younger kids from giggling. Mother Pace was horrified at the behavior and told us, "You are all a disgrace, an embarrassment to the children's home!" She wouldn't let us go to the lido swimming pool outing for punishment. I, too, was embarrassed, but Evelyn and I laughed about it now.

Daddy left attending our school activities up to Dink, but he broke every rule there was to spend more time with us. Though Mother Pace kept reminding him he could only visit on the first Sunday of each month, he would occasionally be parked under the big banyan tree behind the dining room when we got off the bus after school. He would bring watermelons, baskets of fruit, vegetables from the Glades for the cooks to cook, and sometimes boxes of candy bars for kids and staff. He would pat Mother Pace on the shoulder and say, "Mother Pace, I brought several baskets of fresh beans, and the kids and I will sit under this tree back here and get them ready for Maybelle to cook." The boys and girls were not allowed to comingle, so he would take turns having the boys sit under the tree one time and the girls the next. He'd sometimes bring the boys playing cards and marbles, and he showed them how to play root-the-peg with his pocketknife and watched as they played. He said, "There's a few games a boy ought to know." He made a special effort to seek out the troublemakers and spend time with them. All the kids and cooks loved Daddy and were always glad to see him. Mother Pace had no choice but to endure him. It was becoming harder for me to hold on to resentments, to remember how Daddy was when he drank before Mama died, and easier to love the person he had become. There was a time we older kids would have preferred living in the children's home, or the jungle, to living with him, but we were beginning to see what Mama apparently knew about him that we couldn't have known. We were anxious for the day we could get out of the home and live together again.

*****

Dink became certified to sell life insurance. She sold insurance days, and got a night job waitressing at the Pier, a restaurant that extended out over the ocean in Palm Beach. She told us that a lot of teachers and coaches from local schools went there often, and she had met a coach from the high school who also taught industrial arts. She said she didn't like him at first, but he kept teasing her until she learned to like him, and they were dating. He came with her to visit us on the night guests were invited to hear the musicians. He was a big man with a dark tan, a slightly receding hairline of blond-ish hair, and a great smile. She told us he was a swimming coach and spent many hours in the sun. When the musicians played "In the Mood," he asked me to dance. He said Dink told him I could jitterbug. Remembering how Mama made Dink hung a quilt in the hall of our apartment house in Belle Glade, when she and our cousin Charlie practiced jitterbugging to enter competitions, I wasn't about to dance in front of Mother Pace. When I wouldn't dance, Dink stepped over and took his hand, and the kids went crazy, clapping, when they started dancing. He got a unanimous vote from us, but Lois waged a war when they later became engaged.

When school started, we older kids were anxious to ride the bus where boys and girls were not segregated. Paul Sutton, Jimmy Johnson, Carl Armstrong, Charlie Deese, and Roy Nichols, from the home, were some of Northboro Panther's star football, baseball, and basketball players. Evelyn and Paul had a crush on each other, and Jimmy and I had a crush on each other, so as soon as the school bus rounded the corner from the home, we would switch seats to sit next to each other. The athletes rode the bus to school, but Henry would take them home in the home's fifteen-passenger van after practices.

Evelyn and I were teaching the girls cheers and were always practicing with them, and I thought it would be good to have a cheerleader from the home as well. I was shy but got my nerve up to ask Mother Pace if I could try out for cheerleader, to which she quickly answered, "Absolutely not!" The next time Daddy came, I talked to him about how unfair it was. He said, "Well, you need to be respectful to Mother Pace, but sometimes when you know something is unfair, you maybe ought to do something to try to change it."

I said, "What can I do? It's her rule, and she's in charge."

He said, "Didn't you tell me that Lake Lytal tells you kids, when he comes for dinner, to call him if you ever have a problem or need anything? Well, it looks to me like you got a problem…What are you gonna do about it?"

Though Bright Eyes and I, being the oldest girls in the home at that time, were assigned to serve the big round head table at the front of the dining room where Mr. Lytal sat with Mother Pace and others, I couldn't mention it there. I thought about it as I went to bed that night, imagining myself in a blue-and-white cheering outfit, cheering while Jimmy, Paul, Carl, Charlie, and Roy did us proud on the field. I debated with myself if I wanted it bad enough to get in trouble with Mother Pace, who could be a real tyrant. I went to sleep thinking of what Daddy said—that I could be a trailblazer for other girls in the home.

The next day, after school, I didn't catch the school bus to the home. I caught a city bus downtown to the county courthouse. When I entered Commissioner Lytal's office, my knees were shaking. His secretary looked up over her glasses as I walked in and said, "Yes, can I help you?"

I said, "I need to talk to Mr. Lytal. He told us if we ever had any problems to come see him."

"And who may I say wants to see him?"

I could hardly get it out, "Betty Sue from the children's home."

In less than a minute, Mr. Lytal appeared through the door of his office, "Hello, Betty Sue. Good to see you, and what can I do for you today?"

I told him, "I don't think it's fair for the boys at the home to be able to play sports but the girls can't join clubs or go out for any activities that required them to stay after school. I want to go out for cheerleader, and Mother Pace says, 'Girls can't stay after school or go to games.'"

Mr. Lytal stood there smiling and slowly nodding his head as I spoke. He said, "Well, I agree. That's not fair. I'll have a talk with Mother Pace and see how we can make some changes. And…Betty Sue, you are a very brave girl. I'll call Mother Pace so she won't think you ran away."

He had his secretary take me back to the home, and I was shaking as we drove into the big parking lot and parked near the entrance.

Mother Pace was standing on the entrance landing with her hands on her hips and her head cocked back like a bull with steam coming out of his nostrils. Oh boy! I was scared, and as I reached the landing, she caught me by the arm and said, "Don't you *ever* go over my head again, or you'll live to regret it. Get to your dorm."

The day I tried out for cheerleader, I was just as nervous as the day I skipped the bus. I decided I should try something snappy and chose a cheer from the Glades with a bit of hip movement, different from those I learned from Northboro, like "Clap your hands, stamp your feet—get in the rhythm of the boogie, beat-me-daddy, eight-to-the-bar…" I made the cheering team and saw my dream come true. The mother of one of the other cheerleaders, Betty Collum, made my cheering outfit, and sometimes Sisty Robson, another cheerleader, who had her own jeep, would pick me up from the home for games. Maybe I helped bring change, but many of the kids from the home won honors for various accomplishments—Eagle Scouts, captains of sports teams, scholastic honors, etc. Of the ninth-grade graduating class, George Sammons and I won the American Legion Award that year, two students chosen by students and teachers from each school in the country for scholastics, courage, honor, and leadership. Though the children's home was sometimes referred to as the "poor farm," I believe the kids did it proud, and the teachers and classmates from school were great.

The summer had come and gone. I started tenth grade at Palm Beach High School, and I would occasionally see Coach Kehle, whom Dink was dating, in the halls. The kids were all doing good and growing up fast, and we were still in the home. Daddy was up and down with health issues, and we knew it would be too much for him to take on caring for the whole brood again, but he was always there. Besides, we were beginning to feel like all the kids in the home were our brothers and sisters and would feel bad going home when many of them couldn't.

Lois was seventeen, and when she learned Dink and Coach set a date for their wedding, she moved from Dink's apartment to the YWCA and quit school so she could work full-time. Though she didn't get along with Coach, he encouraged her to live with them and finish school. She was very smart and a good student, but she didn't like the way he called her on her teenage rudeness and disobedience to Dink—backtalking, staying past curfew, and loaning Dink's clothes to friends without permission. When she left home, I remember Daddy saying, "She thinks she wants her freedom, but she'll learn that freedom isn't free," something I, too, would later learn.

Dink and the swimming coach got married in a church a week before my sixteenth birthday. We didn't get to go because Evelyn and I were quarantined in the clinic above the nurse's quarters with measles, and since Daddy and Dink were still estranged, there was no one to take the kids. There had been an outbreak, and though we were clear, we were still quarantined through the weekend. We were very disappointed because we wanted to see Lois, who was Dink's maid of honor. Dink said, "You probably wouldn't have seen much of her, because as soon as we said 'I do,' she scuttled out the door."

The next Sunday—my birthday—Dink took us all out of the home to celebrate my sixteenth. She made a big pot of spaghetti and meat sauce loaded with mushrooms. It was the first time I ever ate mushrooms, and I got as sick as a dog. It wasn't the mushrooms—they were delicious—it was the *amount* I ate, plus eating a large piece of Mama's special homemade cake that brought her presence to all our celebrations, with lemon filling and fluffy icing covered with coconut. I made such a pig of myself.

The Monday after my birthday, Daddy was waiting as I got off the school bus to take me to get my permanent driver's license. I didn't notice a 1930s vintage convertible sitting under the tree by the kitchen. After we returned and got out of the old truck he bought to replace our beloved Mule Train, walking toward the old car, he said, "Come take a look at what I got you for your birthday. I know it isn't your favorite color, but I brought some paint remover and red paint, and it will be a good team project for you and the older kids to paint it."

I didn't know what to say or do. I gave him a big hug and said, "Thank you, Daddy, but there's no way Mother Pace will allow me to have a car here." He assured me he would take care of Mother Pace, and I'll never know how, but she allowed me to keep it and even allowed the kids and me to paint it when Daddy was there to supervise. We applied paint remover and scraped paint off with lids from gallon cans of applesauce, beets, and corn. It was the biggest mess you ever saw, but it occupied many hours of our time after school and weekends.

One afternoon we heard one of the cooks, Ethel, yelling at Mother Pace, who was trying to calm her down to no avail. It seems Mother Pace had fired her husband, Henry, who was our driver, and Ethel blew up and quit, so there was no driver to take Maybelle home that night. Mother Pace called me into her office and told me I'd have to drive Maybelle home. Now I learned to drive on tractors and old Mule Train on the ranch and backroads in the Glades, but I had never driven a new fifteen-passenger van, but I swallowed and said, "Yes, ma'am." I hardly got out of the driveway on Forty-Fifth Street, when a policeman pulled me over. I was shaking in my boots when he approached the window of the van and said, "You got a license to drive this, young lady?"

Before I could say anything, Maybelle spoke up, "Yessir, she got a license. Her daddy took her to get it last month."

He said, "Well, let's take a look at your driver's license. Do they know you're driving this?"

Maybelle spoke up again, "Yessir, they knows. Mother Pace told her to bring me home after she fired Henry." The local police all knew Henry, and he raised his eyebrows as he smirked and handed my license back to me. "You be careful and stay safe, Betty Sue. Congratulations on getting your license." I could hardly hold the steering wheel. I was shaking so much. Though she hired another driver, I did a lot of driving for Mother Pace after that day, getting stopped often, until all the local police learned I wasn't running away.

We finally finished our painting project, leaving me with a cherry-red convertible (I say that lightly because the top would hardly go up and down). I couldn't believe Mother Pace allowed me to drive it sometimes, rather than the van, to take Maybelle and the two new cooks, Lottie and Pella, home when the driver was on other errands.

There were things I wanted to buy, like new black-and-white saddle oxfords and fabric to make school clothes for myself and the kids, but I didn't want to accept money from Dink or Daddy. I needed to get a job. Looking at the want ads in Daddy's newspaper, I saw an ad for help in the stockroom of JCPenney's, so I skipped the school bus and walked the few blocks to downtown, and with much more confidence than before, I walked into the office of JCPenney and filled out an application for the job. The lady told me to sit with my application and the manager would see me soon. I was shocked when Uncle Hal walked in, and I realized he was "the manager." I froze. He raised his eyebrows and looked at me, "Betty Sue, what are you doing here. Is anything wrong?"

"I…I…want to apply for this job."

"Does Mother know you're applying for a job?"

"No, sir, not exactly… I thought I'd tell her if I got it."

"Oh my, Betty Sue…I don't think this will go over well with Mother. I think you better talk it over with her first. She doesn't like surprises, you know." He told the lady in the office, "I'll be back in a little while. I need to take her back to the home."

I was busted, but even worse, I had to face Mother Pace and didn't even have a job to show for it. By the time Uncle Hal dropped me off at the front door, Mother Pace already knew and was again waiting on the front stoop with her hands on her hips. Thinking of the times Mama had to be brave, I worked up the courage to call Commissioner Lytal and ask him to help me explain why I wanted to work. He listened as I told him I wanted to pay for my own lunch at school so I wouldn't have to serve other students for free lunches. I remembered what Daddy said about Seabo and saving his dignity, and I felt guilty for feeling vain, but I wanted to stand in line with the other students in the cafeteria. I told him how I wanted to buy Toni's to put perms in for Pricilla and Emily, who didn't have parents, and to buy fabric for our costumes. I don't know what he said to convince Mother Pace, but she allowed me to apply and I got the job. She later confided in me that Uncle Hal told her I was one of the fastest workers he'd ever seen putting tags on clothes in the stockroom. I believe it was all those races picking strawberries and cherries and Daddy's voice in my head every time we started a new job, saying, "Show 'em what you got."

Lulu, Bobby Jean, Bo, & Jesse/children's home

Kids in children's home

Bright Eyes & Buzz perform at pancake benefit

Lois & Dink visit us

Buzz

Dink marries Coach Kehle

Chapter 18

If you find a path with no obstacles, it probably doesn't lead anywhere.
—Frank A. Clark, 1860–1936

After supper each school night, all the kids had to report to the dining room for study hall for an hour. The boys sat around the long tables on the right of the room and girls on the left. I had a habit of occasionally glancing around to spot my siblings, and I noticed Jesse was trying to motion to Evelyn and me to come over to where he and Marion were. We both walked over, and just as we leaned over to see what they needed help with, Carl Armstrong, who had a crush on Evelyn, walked behind us and flicked her on the bottom with the back of his hand—a silly way boys had of flirting in 1953—just as Mother Pace entered the dining room. She grabbed Evelyn by both arms from the back, spun her around, marched her to the room with the bars, and slammed the door. I didn't know what was going on, but I was right behind them. She told me to go back to doing my homework, but I halfway yelled, "What did she do, Mother Pace? We were just helping Marion and Jesse with their homework!" She just stomped back to her office and closed the door. As soon as study hall was over, I scurried across the road to Evelyn's friend and called Dink, because Daddy didn't have a phone. She said, "I'll try to find Daddy and he'll know what to do. It may make it worse if I came tonight, but I'll be there as soon as the doors open in the morning with Daddy."

I couldn't imagine why she locked Evelyn in the pokey rather than Carl, and I didn't sleep, thinking of her being there.

Dink found Daddy at Cusworth's Pub, talking politics with former neighbors and possibly having a drink or two. He was surprised to see her but seemingly pleased. She struggled on occasion with being able to totally forgive him, but she was concerned about how she explained the situation to him, because she knew he was not in good health. She hoped she could convince him to allow Evelyn and me to stay with her and Coach for the time being. He grudgingly agreed that would probably be best for now but assured her it would be temporary, that he was going to find a way to get us all back together. Dink didn't say Daddy had been drinking, and I didn't want to ask, but it was a fear I lived with—that he may start drinking again. Three years had passed, and we had not witnessed him drinking, but two times we *knew* he had been drinking—the night Lois left home and the night he turned Mule Train over in Indiana. I believe we all lived with a tinge of fear and a prayer that he didn't.

Daddy and Dink came early the next morning, and Mother Pace wasn't surprised. She explained to him that we knew we were not allowed on the boys' side, and it was necessary to have everyone adhere to the rules. Daddy told her he didn't like rules that separated sisters and brothers but understood how hard it must be to control eighty-plus kids. When he asked Evelyn and me what we wanted to do, Evelyn quickly answered, "We want to live with Dink." Evelyn and I were so close we often finished each other's sentences, and I couldn't imagine her going anywhere without me, but how would we explain to the kids we were leaving without them? It's still painful remembering—the four of them huddled together as we hugged them and offered the lame excuse that *we were going to find a way to all* be *together again.* Lulu and Bobby Jean started crying, and Bo and Jesse just stood mute with sad faces. I was sick to my stomach and had a bemoaning sense of guilt as we drove away. Remembering how Evelyn and I soothed Lulu's hysterics and Barbara's tears each time Daddy drove away from the home, I was consumed with sadness thinking, *They have no one there to comfort them now.* I almost told Dink to turn around and take me back, but I couldn't let Evelyn go alone. I had always been there to protect her. Once I had to rescue her from an old dog that was almost too old to bark and had no teeth. He scared her so bad she backed into a huge cactus. And another time in Belle Glade, right after Mama died, she and I were going to the store on the corner, when some young migrant men jumped at us from a pile of gravel on the side of the road. I took off running, but when I looked back, Evelyn was frozen in her tracks. I flew back, grabbed her hand, and she outran me to Mrs. Dommer in the store on the corner. She always thought someone was looking through our windows. She needed me.

When we parked near the front door of 216 Beverly Road—a cute angled-roof house a block west of the Intracoastal Waterway on the opposite side of town—Evelyn and I were a bit nervous. Coach, as we called him, wasn't home from swim-team practice when we arrived, and remembering Thanksgiving at Uncle John's, I wondered if Dink had gotten his full approval on such short notice. As we stepped into the living room, there was a welcoming aroma of homemade brownies plus colorful rugs made from rags at each door, a shelf in the tiny kitchen lined with jars of fruits and vegetables, and windows covered with beautiful curtains she had made. She had shifted furniture around in their small well-appointed home to create a bedroom for us. A bed with a new bedspread was squeezed into her sewing room, the small closet emptied, and a vase of orange flowers from her ixora hedge on the nightstand. The rag rugs, colorful filled jars in the kitchen, and curtains reminded me of Mama; it was heart-warming but double bittersweet.

My fears were quelled when Coach arrived with the makings for grilling hamburgers and homemade ice cream. After dinner, we four sat at the picnic table in their little tropical backyard garden with tiki torches and talked, as we shoveled ice and salt into the churn and took turns turning the handle. He seemed content with us being there, expressing interest in our activities and how we were doing in school. Of course, he already knew how I was doing in school, because he knew all my teachers and my grades before I did. Fortunately, I loved school and was a good student. The subject came up about us having to learn new names at the home, and Coach said, "Well, actually, your sister said her name was *Mary Lou*, so maybe she would rather be called her real name." We swiveled our heads toward her; she shrugged and smiled. It was difficult at first, but we were getting pretty good at switching names when we were around him and Mother Pace and when we were at school. Now that we were in high school, Bright Eyes and I were gradually using Evelyn and Betty Sue more but our relatives, many from the home, and close friends called us Bright Eyes and Buzz.

Though Evelyn wasn't in Palm Beach High yet, Coach immediately made us scorekeepers for the swim team so we could ride the bus with him, Mary Lou, and the team to all the out-of-town swim meets. The next season, he got speedos for Evelyn and me, expecting us to join the swim team. Evelyn joined the team, choosing backstroke, but I refused to remove my shirt from over the speedo bathing suit because we were not used to wearing such a tight-fitting bathing suit with no lining in the bra area. I remained a scorekeeper and never learned to be a good swimmer like Evelyn.

The first teens we met in our new neighborhood were JoAnne, Evelyn's age, who lived around the corner from us and attended Palm Beach High; and Mary Jane, a year younger, who lived in a big two-story house across from JoAnne and attended St. Ann's Catholic school. We became fast friends and occasionally caught the city bus into town for a movie. One such time, we were going to meet at Mary Jane's house to walk to the bus stop, and when we got to her house, her older brother, Pat, eighteen and a graduate from St. Ann's High, answered the door. He said, "Hi, JoAnn, come on in. Mary Jane should be down in a couple minutes." He turned to Evelyn and me and said, "I'm Pat, Mary Jane's brother. Aren't you the new girls around the corner on Beverly?" We knew who he was because he often walked his dog, Jill, past our house, and I was already an admirer of his brown and white setter—and now, him too.

JoAnn said, "Yes, this is Betty Sue and Evelyn."

He nodded to each of us. "I'm glad to meet you."

Mary Jane's mother appeared from the kitchen, wiping her hands on a dish towel as she spoke, "Hello, JoAnn. I'm glad to meet you girls too. I'm Jane, Mary Jane and Pat's mom. Having three brothers, Mary Jane is happy to have you girls in the neighborhood."

Mary Jane stuck her head over the bannister from upstairs and, before descending the back steps to the kitchen, yelled, "I'll be a few minutes! I have to empty the dishwasher before I can leave!"

Pat said, "Sis, go. Don't hold the girls up. I'll do it this time." Mary Jane thanked him as we scooted out the door to catch the bus to town.

I couldn't shake the image of Mary Jane's brother Pat. Besides his soft-spoken and polite manner and big friendly smile, he had thick curly brown hair, big hazel-brown eyes, and eyelashes a girl could only dream of having. Of all my guy friends on athletic teams and in classes, none had captured my attention and feelings as he did.

That night, I told Evelyn, "I really like Mary Jane's brother. If I *ever* marry, that's the kind of guy I hope to marry." She was surprised because I had been getting calls from guys from school and always made excuses, but Coach was always teasing me about being shy, and saying he was going to find a great guy for me. I suspected him of putting guys up to calling me so I wouldn't accept a date with any guys from Palm Beach High.

We missed seeing our younger siblings, but we visited them as often as transportation and time allowed. I was not allowed to keep my car because there was only room for parking the little Hillman that Mary Lou drove and the older woody that Coach drove in their small driveway. I'll admit I wouldn't blame Coach if it may have had something to do with how ridiculous my car looked, as well. I honestly wonder sometimes if Daddy had "keeping me humble" in mind when he gave it to me and planned the paint project. Mary Lou, Evelyn, and I attended the Wednesday nights for guests at the home with the musicians, and though I wasn't sure we would be welcomed, Mother Pace was cordial when we visited afterward. We always felt let down and talked at night about how frustrated we were when the kids told us they were being picked on or roughed up by a few bad kids in the home, and threatened with consequences if they tattled. We just had to find a way to get them out.

Lois was eighteen, living at the YWCA, having the time of her life. The Officer's Club at Palm Beach Air Force Base in West Palm Beach sent buses to transport local single ladies, including those at the YWCA, to attend dances on the base. Many local girls were marrying guys from the base, and though Lois loved dancing with them, she soon became engaged to a sailor, Dale Nelson, a prior boyfriend's older brother, who was home on leave. It was crazy, but she called Mary Lou while we were in school one day and asked her to come to the West Side Baptist Church rectory, because she needed her to be a witness for her and Dale to marry. Only Mary Lou and the minister who married them were present when they said their vows. Mary Lou asked her if she was pregnant, and she quickly said, in her persnickety way, "Hell no! We just decided to get married before Dale returns from leave." She had passed a test for her GED (general education diploma) and was taking accounting classes at the local college and working two jobs. This was the same Lois who always found a way to get out of work, whom Daddy teased by saying, "Lois is not afraid of work. She can lie right down by it and go to sleep." She must have been storing her energy for years. She was a whirlwind and busier than ever. We were somehow seeing a little more of her, but she was still unrelenting about voicing her hate for Daddy.

When Mack came home on leave, we were so excited we took him to the home to see the kids—pretty much as we had learned from Daddy—with no notice. Mother Pace called Jesse, Marion, Bobby Jean, and Shirley on the speaker to go to report to the big room. They were so happy and excited when they saw Mack with us. She allowed us to take the kids to the pavilion and visit for a long time. When Barbara saw Mack's harmonica in his pocket, where it usually stayed, she asked him to play. When he started playing, boys and girls gathered from all directions, and Mother Pace sent Mrs. Sanford to the pavilion to supervise but didn't separate them. He must have practiced many hours in his army bunk, because he made that harmonica sing. He played a song that sounded like a train was coming at us, and the kids loved it. Hearing the train whistle conjured up a sad memory of Mama's abuse while living by the tracks in Pahokee, but it was quickly replaced with thoughts of how proud Mother would be, and we were, of our harmonica-playing Green Beret. I was beginning to be able to blur sad memories and feelings with new, happy ones being made. Mother Pace allowed us to visit until the dinner bell rang. She asked if we wanted to join the kids for dinner, but Mary Lou was expecting us home. I was very fond of Mother Pace and regretted the previous rift between us. I believe Daddy must have smoothed it over with her, as he was a champion peacemaker, and the way she treated us made me feel as if she regretted it as well.

Coach was an avid fisherman, and when he wasn't assisting with the football team at games, coaching at swim meets, or in the classroom, he was fishing. Jesse and Bo loved him because he taught them how to fish in brackish and saltwater. When we brought them from the home, if it didn't conflict with Daddy's plans, we would go to the beach with a picnic under the Southern Boulevard Bridge, next to where President Trump's Mar Largo now sits, and the guys would fish while Mary Lou, Evelyn, and I worked on our tans and Barbara and Shirley played in the water.

We had become close friends with JoAnn and Mary Jane, so when Mary Jane told us JoAnn's mom was giving a party for Pat's nineteenth birthday, we were looking forward to attending, but days passed with no mention of the party from JoAnn. It was a jolt when we learned that though we were not invited, a couple of other neighbors and JoAnn's cousin Vivian were. She didn't even know Pat. Mary Jane told us she thought the purpose of the party was for JoAnn's cousin to meet Pat. I was surprised to receive a call from Pat a couple of weeks later, asking me to go to a movie, and I accepted because I knew Coach could not have put him up to calling me. We continued dating, and after a few months, he gave me his class ring.

With one riff settled, another storm was brewing. Coach didn't want Evelyn and me to go with Daddy to help him at the humongous garden he planted on acreage owned by Uncle John. We would go every chance we could between school and activities to help him tend his garden, pick vegetables, and sell produce with him at his stand in town. I'm sure Coach knew, at least a little, about the challenges Mary Lou had incurred with Daddy and about our working as migrants, all of which he disapproved. He told us, "It isn't *lady-like* for girls to be working on a farm." Like most people, it was a different world to him, and we couldn't expect him to understand why we loved working and spending time with Daddy. When we returned from a day with Daddy with muck smudged on us and our clothes, Coach expressed his objections and criticized Daddy's judgment. This created a chasm between him and me, and sometimes between him and Mary Lou, when she felt he was being too critical of the situation. We knew, in spite of her differences with Daddy, if circumstances were different, she, too, would be helping Daddy as well.

Evelyn was now a sophomore at Palm Beach High, and I a junior. We were both cheerleaders on the junior varsity team. We were at a game one night, when I saw Daddy walking in front of the bleachers toward the area where we were cheering. It scared me. I thought something was wrong, and we both broke from the line and ran toward him. He said, "Hey, Buzz, Bright Eyes, I thought it was time I came to see you do your cheers." We were relieved that nothing was wrong but puzzled that he would be there. He never came to our activities after we left the Glades and Mary Lou filled that role, and for a minute, I was embarrassed. He was wearing his dirty farm clothes, stained felt hat, and shoes that looked like they belonged to a homeless man. By now the cheerleaders and other friends in front were looking to see what was wrong, but we gave him a hug, took a deep breath, and each took one of his hands to go meet the other cheerleaders. I was on to his many ways of teaching us humility. I said, "I want y'all to meet Daddy. Daddy, this is Sisty, Betty…" etc. He took off his hat and said, "I'm mighty glad to meet you, ladies. You're doing a good job there with your cheerleading." They were all great. They shook his hand and gave him their full attention. Daddy sat right in front of us and watched until halftime, then he came over and told me he needed to get back home. *He had taught his lesson for the day.* I believed he was testing to see if we were getting hoity-toity on him. We later laughed.

Coach wanted Dink to give up her job. He wanted her to be available to meet him for lunch or to go fishing with him at the drop of a hat. He was a good-hearted guy, but his German culture, where the man of the house held all the purse strings and called all the shots in the family, was beginning to get a little pushback from Mary Lou, as he started laying down the law and putting rules in place before discussing with her. We weren't allowed to talk to him until he had his second cup of coffee each morning. Evelyn and I were not allowed to do anything in the kitchen except wash dishes—Mary Lou would do all the cooking. If she wanted me to run an errand for her, he said I couldn't drive her car; and when I wanted to get a job, he said he would have to approve before I could apply. One day she blew up and, in spite of him insisting she couldn't work, took a job as a police patrol at the elementary school around the corner from their house and opened her own bank account. Coach laughingly told his fellow coaches about the firecracker he married and actually began to loosen up on some things.

Jobs were hard to come by, but Coach got upset when I accepted a job without his approval at Kings—an enclosed flea market with individuals selling a wide variety of new and used things from bins and booths. I earned ten dollars a week working for an older couple from the garment industry in New York, selling seconds from a men's clothing factory. Coach was gracious, providing us with a home and showing concern about our well-being, but I was beginning to think, since I was seventeen, I should be paddling my own canoe. Very few things bothered me, but Coach's disapproval of Daddy was getting to me. After one such encounter, I moved to a room at the YWCA for three dollars a week, plus fifty cents to use the refrigerator and kitchen. I scurried to my job after school, and Pat picked me up when I got off a little after nine at night and took me to Barrow's Root Beer Stand to eat, before driving me to the YWCA. I always ordered a bowl of chili, which was about the least expensive and most filling item on menu, because I knew Pat would be paying. Mary Lou often brought me groceries she scrounged from her cabinets and money she made selling potted plants she rooted. I wouldn't accept money but gladly took the groceries.

Evelyn and I were always concerned about how things were going for the kids in the home without us there, and when Evelyn would hear of incidents at school, it was upsetting. There were two girls in their dormitory who were repeatedly running away from home. They had lived on the streets and tried to act tough. Barbara said they tried to make her lick blood off a scratch on one of their arms, but Shirley told Mother Pace and they got in trouble. Another time, the "Bossy twins," as the kids called them, tried to push Barbara's face in the sand. That would never have happened if we were there. When Jesse started attempting to run away from the home too, Daddy fired up efforts to get them out. Besides his produce business, he bought an old dump truck and started hauling dirt and rock and accumulated enough money to rent a house in West Gate. Like many men in 1953, our half brother Ithaniel was struggling to get full-time work, so Daddy made a win-win deal with him and his wife, Bert. Ithaniel could help Daddy part-time; Bert would help with the kids, and Daddy would pay the rent. Bert had been close with Mama, and we loved her. She was great with kids, loved to cook, and welcomed the deal.

It was a happy day when Daddy picked me up at the Y, and Evelyn from Dink's, and we drove away from the children's home for the last time, packed like sardines, laughing and crying in the cab of Daddy's dump truck.

Thanks to Dink's forgiving heart—remembering Mama's last wish for her to get along with Daddy, and Daddy's herculean effort to fulfill Mama's wish to keep us together and make amends—Dink had come to terms with much of the pain he had caused before Mama died. Lois had a more mature attitude toward Coach but still held a grudge against Daddy and would not participate with what we had come to call our "Daddy adventures."

The Saturday night after we took the kids out of the home, to celebrate, he took us to one of our favorite places—a barn dance at Wellman's. It was a huge rustic building where weekly family square dances were held with live music by The Florida Trailblazers. Lois stayed home with Baby Wayne while Dale, her husband, worked the night shift as a fireman. Daddy knew the guys in the band, and of course, he got Bobby Jean, Lulu, Bright Eyes, and me up to sing. We square-danced and danced with each other until the band stopped playing at eleven. We kept asking Daddy if he was ready to go, because we could tell he wasn't feeling too good, but he insisted on staying. He took us to the Okeechobee Steakhouse for hamburgers and Cokes, then we all spent the night on pallets that our brother's wife had made up for us. We awoke the next morning to the smell of Bert's biscuits and sounds of Daddy in the kitchen cooking bacon and eggs. It felt great for the kids to be out of the home and for us to be with the kids again.

Lois at beach

Verna & Mack, home on leave

Bo, Coach, & Bright Eyes

Jesse with fish

Bo the fisherman

Dink & Daddy talk

Chapter 19

Sometimes it's the journey that teaches you about your destination.

—Drake

Daddy asked Bert to make sure the girls continued going to church, like they did in the home, so Bobby Jean and Lulu caught the bus to the West Side Baptist Church every Sunday morning. They had only attended three or four times when Bobby Jean decided she wanted to be baptized. She told Daddy she was going to be baptized the next Sunday and she wanted him to be there. As expected, he said, "That church will fall in on everyone if I go inside, Bobby Jean."

"Well then, I just won't get baptized."

"No, you need to get baptized. Your mama would want you to."

"Not if you don't come, Daddy."

"Now, Bobby Jean, you don't need me there to get dipped in that tank," but he finally promised he would attend, and I held my breath. I never figured out why he was opposed to being in a church, but I hoped he would get over it and not disappoint her. He was raised to attend church several times a week and would always point out to us the miracles of nature—how a little acorn became a massive tree, and a handful of seeds could become a garden of vegetable big enough to feed a neighborhood. He once said, "I know there's a higher power holding the universe together and making things happen, but I don't know about its being a man with long hair, wearing a dress and sandals."

That Sunday morning, Dink, Evelyn, and I were sitting near the front. We kept looking back toward the door. I was praying Daddy wouldn't let Bobby Jean down. She wouldn't understand.

I couldn't believe it, but when Brother Lamerson's services started with him standing in the baptismal font in the front of the little church, and Bobby Jean second in line to be immersed, Daddy was sitting in the back pew. He disappeared as soon as Bobby Jean was baptized, but we truly witnessed a miracle that Sunday morning.

A couple months passed, and Bert told Daddy she wasn't happy with the school the kids were attending or the behavior of the kids in the neighborhood. Aunt Rhodie told Bert her daughter Lily Mae was living in the south end of West Palm Beach and was real happy with the school. As luck would have it, there was a house for rent next door to her, so Daddy rented it, and they moved. Lily Mae had children our kids' ages, and they were happy to have "relatives" for neighbors. But one day Bobby Jean ran home crying hysterically. One of the older kids had told her, "Your Daddy killed your mama."

Bert marched right over to see Lily Mae to deal with the situation and demanded, "Where in the world did these young kids hear such a thing? Their mama bled to death when she fell on her stomach with her twelfth baby in her stomach and a worn-out body!" This was a most painful thing for Bert to convey to Dink and us girls.

We had become very close to Bert, and she knew we older kids had made a pact before we left Belle Glade to never talk about Daddy's abuse and drinking or say bad things about him around the kids, who were too young to remember. We knew Mama would want it that way. We wanted them to know and remember the best of him. *They* had never known him to be anything but loving, caring, and totally dedicated to the well-being of all of us.

Lily Mae's daughter apologized and said she didn't mean it, but it sent us into a tailspin to think *that was what some were thinking.* We were not prepared to know how to handle such a painful situation or deal with the rekindled memories. We, of course, did not tell Daddy, and we told Bobby Jean not to mention it. We told her, "Sometimes kids will make up the meanest things they can think of, but she didn't mean it." Daddy would have told her what he told us when we complained if someone was being mean: "Time to me this truth has taught, 'tis a lesson worth revealing, more often from lack of thought than ever lack of feeling." We could only pray for guidance if this was what we would be dealing with.

Only days passed when there was another crisis. Ithaniel spanked Lulu for something she said she didn't do. Now, Lulu had learned to take up for herself and Barbara in the home. As sweet and caring as she was, she could be spunky. She once chased a dog, after he nipped her, and bit his tail, so it's possible she *could* have been guilty of slamming their son, Willard, who had a mean streak. Daddy got upset over it; he had made it clear that he must be consulted if the kids needed to be disciplined. He started feeling pains down his arm and in his chest and ended back in the emergency room.

Although Lois had just given birth to a new son, she wanted Bo and Jesse to stay with her and Dale. Dolly and Jake Taylor, who helped with us after Mama died, had moved to West Palm Beach and offered to take Bobby Jean and Lulu with them until Daddy got better.

Daddy was out of the hospital in three days, but we quickly put our heads together to avoid the kids returning next door to Lily Mae's kids. The boys were with Lois, the girls were with Dolly, and we urged Daddy to leave them there until he was stronger. He reluctantly agreed.

Evelyn and I took turns riding the city bus to the north end after school, one day each week, in between Dink's visits, to help Lois. One day, I had just arrived at Lois's little apartment, which had been converted from a detached garage behind an older lady's home, when we heard a pop of glass breaking and yelps from Jesse and Bo near the back door in the yard. Lois and I flew outside to find they had mixed some of her hair developer in a quart jar, shook it up, and it exploded, sending them thrashing through a beautiful flower bed with a trail of broken glass and hair bleach behind. We grabbed them and hosed them in the face and all over. Miraculously, none got in their eyes, and thank heavens, they were not injured; however, Lois feared she would get evicted over the destruction of Mrs. Bailey's flower garden. I know Mother must have been watching them when we weren't, but I believe she was glad we were slowly getting some of the missing parts back together.

Lois's marriage began to deteriorate because she was working two, sometimes three jobs, and Dale didn't seem to be able to keep one. Daddy rented the apartment over Johnny Wooten's Auto Repair Shop just outside town and took all four kids to live with him. He seemed to get a sudden burst of energy with the kids being under his roof, and his produce and dump truck was making enough to pay rent and buy groceries.

That Thanksgiving, Daddy cooked a big turkey with oyster stuffing, black-eyed peas with ham hock and okra, fresh corn, cornbread, and fresh tomatoes for a kind of a mandatory family gathering. Each time I saw him before Thanksgiving, he would tell me, "I expect you to bring that fella you have for Thanksgiving now."

I avoided introducing them because I knew Daddy would embarrass him, but in the meantime, Pat was also asking, "When do I get to meet your dad?" so I bit the bullet and invited him, though I knew everything including black-eyed peas and okra would be strange to him.

As we got out of the car when we arrived at Wooten's Garage on Thanksgiving, we stepped around huge patches of oil on the ground and dodged old radiators and abandoned auto parts to reach the concrete stairs on the side of the building. Climbing the stairs with dread, I took a deep breath as we reached the landing, before opening the door. I was touched to see the special effort Daddy had made. There was a stack of matching plates and glasses at the end of the counter, not our usual mishmash of dishes and jelly glasses, but I knew the worst was yet to come. I wasn't surprised when I introduced Pat to Daddy, and he said, "I'm glad to meet you, son, and I have a question for you. What are your plans with my daughter, Buzz? Are you thinking about marrying her?" Pat and I had hardly gotten past the stage of holding hands. I was so embarrassed I could have jumped out the two-story window.

But you could have knocked me over with a feather when Pat answered, "Yes, actually, I was eventually going to talk to you about that, Mr. Meeks." Now, that was how he proposed to me! On the way home, he told me, "Your dad thought he'd scare me off, but I was on to him from the beginning, and I knew from the first date with you, I would ask you to marry me." I told him I wasn't ready to marry, that

I wanted to see my younger siblings become old enough to care for themselves. He said we could help take care of them together, but I knew how impractical that was to think about at that time.

I continued trudging to the flea market after school on foot, and Pat continued picking me up from work and taking me to the YWCA after a bowl of chili. I was having a challenge stretching my ten-dollar paycheck from week to week. I would buy six pot pies at three for a dollar, a package of bologna, a loaf of bread, a jar of peanut butter, and a jar of jelly for my weeks' supply of food; and by the time I paid $3.50 rent and $0.50 to use the refrigerator/freezer at the YWCA, I was broke and too proud to let anyone know. The problem was, though I hid my bread, peanut butter, and jelly in my room, when I returned to the freezer to get a potpie or slice of bologna for a sandwich, someone hungrier than I would have taken it. Though I knew I could, I didn't want to swallow my pride and move back in with Dink and Coach or pile in on Daddy, so I canceled use of the kitchen, saving fifty cents, and bought food I could hide in my room, like Vienna sausage. I was still looking for a better-paying job but knew if I could hold out until school was over, I could work more hours and improve my situation. Thinking of Mama's challenges, I knew it could be worse.

In the meantime, my guardian angel, who I would always believe was Mama, stepped in. Southern Bell Telephone Company went on strike, and Mr. Jenkins, Pat's neighbor and JoAnn's dad, happened to ask Pat if he knew anyone who would be willing to cross a picket line to work. He asked me. I gladly applied and was hired for after school and weekends as a long-distance telephone operator. Pat no longer had to take me home after work. I was accompanied by a guard in a cab after each day's work. When I was spit at and called a scab as I entered the building downtown, my need created courage and diminished my fear. I stashed every extra penny I could, as I figured it was only be a matter of time before I would be looking for another job. I was surprised to learn from my floor superintendent that the district manager, Mr. Jenkins, and other managers were plugging into my board, after being told I always seemed to keep my board filled. She told me they were surprised that I, a high school student, was taking more calls than some of the regular switchboard operators, but they had not picked as many strawberries, cherries, beans, and tomatoes as I had. That was another time I realized Daddy was right. Nothing we learned in life was wasted. The strike that started in March ended after sixty-eight days near the end of May, and I was thankful I was asked to remain working after school and weekends.

Our four younger siblings were bounced from one place to another when Daddy would end up in the hospital with his heart problem or other health issues. He bought a little house west of town on a land contract to assure the kids would have a place to live in case anything happened to him. Dink, Evelyn, and I took turns going out to check on him, clean, and help the kids however we could.

Jesse was eleven by now, and Daddy taught him to drive the dump truck, and all he wanted to do was drive on the back roads and help Daddy work on the truck to keep it running. We were all excited that Mack didn't sign up for another tour in the Army and would be coming home. Jesse was especially happy, because he remembered how much Mack loved working on cars. Bo would rather go fishing, and the girls stayed busy with music and singing lessons.

Evelyn and I had been active in high school during her sopho-more and my junior year. We were both officers for various clubs, she more than me, and we were junior varsity cheerleaders when Buddy "Burt" Reynolds was on Palm Beach High's varsity football team.

Pat bought his first car, a black 1955 Bellaire Chevrolet coupe, and started talking about his next goal—to marry me and make plans for our future. I told him I couldn't even think about getting married until I made sure we older siblings helped Daddy raise our younger ones. He insisted we could be more help if we were married and worked on it together. I didn't want to put such a responsibility on him, but he insisted he wanted nothing more than to be a part of my life. I was so in love with this kind-hearted, good man I had been dating for two years, but this made me love him even more, because I knew he meant every word of what he said.

We became engaged in June and set the date for August 27 that summer. Pat would be twenty-one, and I, almost nineteen. We made plans to be married in St. Juliana Catholic Church, and I began catechism classes to be baptized Catholic, as I wanted to have a common faith with him. I purchased a beautiful dusty-blue silk dress and shoes to be dyed to match for Evelyn to be my maid of honor, and clothes for Daddy to walk me down the aisle—dress pants and white shirt, no coat and tie. Pat's brother, Jack, would be his best man.

Dink spent many hours on many nights making my wedding dress, veil, and lace gloves. The reception would be in Pat's family's home. I was baptized Catholic, and everything was going smooth as planned—until a big upset the week before the wedding, when Father Bucco informed us that Evelyn could not be in my wedding because she was not Catholic. I simply didn't want to get married without her in my wedding; we had been through so much together and had become so close we finished each other's sentences. I was heartbroken and didn't know how I was going to tell her, and when I did, she took the little money she had saved for a ticket on a Greyhound bus to Granny's in North Florida. I was devastated but tried to create the least upset after everyone's work on Pat and my behalf. The joy of my wedding was shattered, but I forged ahead, helping Mary Lou and Lois sew sequins and pearls on my veil and Mary Lou, Pat's mom, and neighbors make tea sandwiches, cream puffs, and other treats to be frozen until our reception. I asked Mary Jane to be my maid of honor. She was too petite to wear the dress and shoes I bought, so her mom quickly made her a blue dress and purchased matching shoes and hat.

On the big day, everyone was seated in the church, including Mother Pace, Mrs. Sanford, a few of the older kids from the home, Nell Smith, Lake Lytal, a few friends from high school, neighbors, and all my siblings. It was raining so hard I had to wait in the car until it slowed enough to dash to the church. We were running late, but Daddy had not arrived, and it was getting awkward. We waited and waited, but he never came!

I knew he kept saying the church would cave in, but he'd finally agreed to walk me down the aisle if he didn't have to wear a coat and tie, and I had never known him to break a promise. I was sick to my stomach. What if he'd had another heart attack?

I made a mistake I will always regret. I didn't want to have Coach give me away and criticize Daddy for not showing, so in my state of extreme fear, hurt, and disappointment, when Pat's dad offered to walk me down the aisle, I thanked him, took his arm, held my head up, and started walking toward the altar where Pat was waiting. Thinking about it later, I was ashamed I didn't ask Coach, who had been so good to me, and felt guilty realizing I was harboring resentment toward him.

At the reception in the beautiful spacious home of Pat's parents, his mom, Dink, and neighbors Mrs. Jenkins and Margaret Siemon had worked hard to make everything perfect. There were flowers on the mantel, tables, and buffet, and with a generous spread of food on the big dining table and buffet and free-flowing drinks and champagne, it should have been a perfect day. In spite of a sense of emptiness without Evelyn, I had a sense of everything being so right. My heart overflowed with love and appreciation for the support of so many and for the person with whom I knew I would spend the rest of my life. When the telephone rang, Pat motioned for me to come to the phone. It was Evelyn. "Buzz, I'm sorry I ran off the way I did. I really wish I would have been at your wedding and could be there with you now."

"It's all right. Don't worry. It's good to talk to you, and I can't wait to hear about everybody up there. When are you coming home?"

"I'll be home next week before school starts. I don't have any more change for the phone, so I gotta run, but I love you, and congratulations."

"I can't wait. I love you too. Bye."

I felt much better, having talked to her. In the meantime, my brother Mack had found Daddy and told me, "He's okay, he just got cold feet." I should have known when he didn't come to the practice the night before; he said, "I don't know why you need to 'practice' a wedding. I'll just wait for the real thing."

Bobby Jean and Lulu were in awe at the wedding and reception, but though I'm quite sure Jesse and Bo could hardly wait until Mass ended, they had a good time hurling rice at us as we walked out. They all enjoyed the fancy sandwiches and punch, and the boys really got into helping to tie tin cans, shoes, and crazy items to the back of Pat's car.

Before we left the reception to go to Fort Lauderdale for the weekend, Pat was tipped off that some of his buddies had arranged for us to be stopped by police friends of theirs when we drove south through Lake Worth. When we left, the kids squealed with joy as they ran behind the car for almost a block as we headed south. Pat suddenly did a U-turn and headed north, opposite of where we had previously planned. I asked him if plans had changed, and he said, "You'll see," as he continued driving north. We were in Daytona Beach, before he told me we were going to Panama City to see Evelyn. Since we both had to be back to work Tuesday, I couldn't believe he would drive over a thousand miles in two days for me to see her. This man had to be the most thoughtful, caring man in the world, and I reveled in knowing I would spend the rest of my life with such a human. When we got to Millville the next day, Evelyn was so happy to see us, and we had a great visit while Pat chatted with Granny. It was the first time I had seen Granny in seven years, since Mama's funeral. It was as if it was only a short time. She was very happy to see me, and I to see her. She cooked up about everything in the house to make sure there was something Pat liked and told me she could tell he was a special person. I didn't tell her he was Catholic, because I remembered her saying they worshiped idols, and we should stay away from them. I smiled to myself, remembering Mama saying Granny meant well, that she had just grown up being misinformed about many things, like not dancing or singing certain songs around Granny. I didn't tell her about *my* becoming a Catholic. I wondered why we didn't talk about Mama. Maybe it was still painful for her, but I think Mama was happy we saw her.

I got to thinking about why Daddy didn't show, and as I thought of Mama, it made it hard to be angry with him. Maybe he had some residual beliefs he had never talked about when he realized he would be in a Catholic church, but when I told him I was taking catechism, to have the same religion as Pat, he said, "One religion is about as good or bad as another—mostly good for social purposes—and keeps a lot of people out of trouble." Maybe he knew Coach was raised Catholic and would know what to do, that it would be better if he walked me down the aisle if he didn't show. But more likely, he had taken a drink or two. I had to stop thinking about it and let it go.

After I got over the initial anger, I asked him, "Daddy, why didn't you come to my wedding? You said you would!"

He looked down at his feet and said, "I didn't know that Latin stuff, and I just didn't want to embarrass you."

I said, "Well…?" And when I saw he looked so contrite and didn't know what to say, I teased, "Well, I'm sure glad it was *you* and *not* Pat who got cold feet."

Buzz & Bright Eyes

Betty marries Pat

Chapter 20

No winter lasts forever; no spring skips its turn.
—Hal Borland

Pat and I had a cute efficiency apartment over a garage behind a house in the Flamingo District, a block from an apartment Lois, Dale, and Baby Wayne had recently moved into. Evelyn returned from Granny's, and she and I resumed finishing each other's sentences. All four kids and Mack, now home from the Army, were living with Daddy in their new home. They planted a garden, and Daddy bought some chickens and rabbits to occupy the kids, and Mack had acquired a couple of old jalopies for him and Jesse to work on. We girls, now including Lois, continued taking turns checking on them. Dink had helped navigate most of us onto safe ground, and with us having babies, she wanted a baby of her own. Learning that wasn't to be, she and Coach applied to adopt and had just learned they were approved to become adoptive parents. We were all excited, and I couldn't help but think, *Mama would be so happy for Dink. She would be happy for Pat and me, and love that Daddy and the kids are back together.*

*****

I had been dreading the first day of Evelyn's junior and my senior year. She and I met before class at the campus shop, where everyone hung out in front of Palm Beach High. I had butterflies in my stomach as the crowd of classmates grew around us. Since my getting married was unexpected for many classmates, it would be the buzz around campus for a few days, but I was never so certain that marrying Pat was the best choice I had ever made. Though I would be nineteen in December, older than many seniors, I wanted to graduate with my class and register for evening college classes. With a December birthday, I started school late, and I was held back the year after Mama died for missing too much school. It was reassuring to see several other married students attending classes and even two who were expecting. It had to be embarrassing for Evelyn, because some students and teachers, thinking we were twins, confused us for each other, and she would occasionally have someone congratulate her or want to know more about whom she married. There was even an ad for First Federal Savings in our yearbook with Evelyn and me holding a sign saying, "We repeat, 3% interest."

Evelyn was in the choir and elected secretary of her class, cheerleader, and "most friendly" for her junior yearbook. We participated in an occasional singing engagement, but I didn't participate in school activities. My focus was on Pat and our plan to become more helpful with the kids. I was lucky that Southern Bell kept me on after the strike for after school and weekends. Pat was an apprentice, installing plumbing in hospitals and schools with an industrial mechanical contractor, and he attended classes two nights each week. We were happy and optimistic about our future.

The air was alive with holiday spirit. With our neighbors' homes adorned with decorated Christmas trees and garland and reindeer and sleighs twinkling with lights on manicured lawns, I envisioned the day Pat and I would have our own home to decorate for the holidays. We had just returned from delivering Christmas cookies to Lois, Dink, Daddy, and the kids. Christmas music was playing on the radio. I was sprinkling coconut over the fluffy icing on Mama's special cake, when I became sick to my stomach. I made a dash for the toilet, thinking I had overindulged eating goodies, but I would later learn I was two months pregnant. This was not what we planned. Apparently, I had inherited Mama's DNA for fertility—and using the unreliable rhythm method for birth control, we should not have been surprised. Two months after learning that I was expecting, Dink and Coach adopted a beautiful baby boy they named Rodney. We were hoping I would have a boy to be his playmate.

The telephone company was still hiring full-time switchboard operators, so against all my teachers' and Daddy's wishes, I took the test for my GED (general education diploma) and became a full-time long-distance telephone operator with Southern Bell. Education to be continued after the baby.

I was ordered to bed rest for an undetermined time and was unable to work, so we had to back up and punt. I couldn't remember a time I couldn't come up with some solution for a problem. We moved in with Pat's parents, in the bedroom upstairs that had been vacant since Jack left for college and Pat got married, as his Mom and Dad insisted we do. They had tried to convince Pat not to marry at age twenty-one, but once we made plans, they welcomed me lovingly into the family and seemed proud of our determination. I *did not* want to be a burden to anyone, but I had no oars for paddling my own canoe this time. It was humbling.

It was comforting to know we were just around the corner from Dink and Evelyn. Everyone went out of their way to care for me, including Mom's maid, Alzaline, who was always flitting around me. I couldn't have felt more loved, but it was so frustrating feeling so helpless. Mary Jane would always come up to check on me when she got home from school, and I always knew Pat's youngest brother Mike was home when a whiff of hamburger floated up the back stairwell. He loved to eat and would pop a hamburger in the pan the minute he came in the back door and dropped his books. Mike was the jolliest, chubby eleven-year-old ever and fun to have around.

At night, lying beside Pat, I felt secure. Every night I had a recurring dream where Mama was at the foot of my bed, assuring me, as she had so many times before—after the shotgun incident, when the deputies with guns took the jugs, after Daddy's abuse, etc.— "Don't be afraid. Everything will be okay," but once daylight came and I awoke, I never felt more insecure and scared.

Every time I tried to do something for myself, Mom would say, "You're supposed to be resting to take care of our baby. She and Dad were over the top with excitement about their first grandbaby. She made a special effort to have nutritious meals and cooked things she had never cooked before, like turnips and black-eyed peas, thinking I would eat better and feel more at home.

After two months at Mom and Dad's, I was up and around and felt like I could lick the world, but Mom wouldn't let me lift a finger. Dr. Rowe said I couldn't go back to work until after I had the baby but was confident we were both on safe ground.

When Pat received a good raise after being made supervisor on a big school construction job, we started thinking about an apartment of our own. Mom and Dad would not let us pay for anything, and I was beginning to feel like we should start paddling. We had saved almost every penny, except for paying car payments, fuel, and insurance for the car. I penciled a budget and showed it to Pat. "I'm sure we can manage to pay our car payment, utilities, and groceries if we can find an apartment for forty-five dollars month."

He had observed me squeezing pennies for a while and said, "If you think we can make it, I think we should go for it."

Dink was an expert at finding a good deal on rentals, and we set out to find one. It took a few days, but we found a spacious one-bedroom with an alcove sleeping area and big kitchen that was completely furnished. It was on the second floor of an old apartment house and looked down onto an enclosed patio that separated it from another two-story building. The manager who showed it to us was a middle-aged Italian lady. Thinking she might hesitate to rent to a "Buzz" or a "Dink," I said, "I'm Betty Sue, and this is my sister, Mary Lou." She said her name was Rose. After seeing the apartment and learning the rent was fifty-five dollars, we thanked her and turned to leave. She said, "Wait a minute Sue. How much rent *can* you pay?"

When I shrugged my shoulders and answered, "Forty-five dollars," I couldn't believe she said, "I'd like you to have that apartment. It's yours for forty-five dollars."

Now for the hard part…telling Mom and Dad.

Actually, Mom and Dad were great. Though they attempted to talk us out of moving out, I believe they were proud of our resolve to make it on our own. Early Saturday morning, Dink and Evelyn arrived early to pack clothes and stacks of wedding gifts stored in the closet. In a matter of a couple of hours, we were all moved; dishes, pots, and pans washed; and our few belongings cleaned and set up in our new apartment, including the eleven-inch black-and-white TV console that Coach's sister gave us. Dink made a delicious casserole with Coach's catch and a salad, so I didn't need to cook dinner when Pat came home.

Despite the squeaky budget, we loved having our own apartment. We made car payments on the new car, but there was no money for leisure driving. The car was parked except when Pat drove to work or I to doctor appointments. Fortunately, Publix was only a block away, and we walked a few blocks to the park and watched Little League and Peanut League games for entertainment. When Bobby Jean and Lulu came on weekends, which was often, we baked cookies, played cards, and worked on their routines, but the boys were happy staying home with Daddy, learning mechanics and fishing.

We were all concerned about Jesse. He was thirteen and had skipped so much school hanging out at Johnny Arant's Junkyard, playing with engines and auto parts. He failed eighth grade. But Coach Cushman, who oversaw the summer school program and was a good friend of Dink's husband, told us that if we could get him to attend classes—he didn't have to do any work, just attend—he would pass him. He said Jesse was smart and just going through a "teenage" stage. Jesse was a quiet one with huge, innocent-looking blue eyes. He was brilliant and never caused any trouble but was as stubborn as a mule. Pat suggested, "Mr. Meeks, we have room for Jesse to live with us, and Betty can take him to school." Daddy looked relieved and quickly agreed, so each morning I drove Pat twenty-five miles to work and took Jesse to Central Junior High and dropped him off for class. By the time I got back to our apartment, Jesse was with his buddies at a swimming hole a few blocks away where boys swam in the nude and he knew I would not go.

We couldn't reason with him. He wanted to be back at Daddy's working on cars, but Daddy laid down the law and said if he didn't go to school, he was on his own. Pat and I were perplexed. What did we know about raising a thirteen-year-old? When we put him on restriction, he'd take his sketch pad to bed and sketch cars. One night, we were feeling bad about him being grounded, so we gathered change and went to get him up to go for ice cream. We found his bed padded with pillows and no Jesse. We found him on his bike, surrounded with kids at the baseball park. This became his routine. We were concerned and exasperated and decided we had to lay down the law too. Pat said, "Jesse, if you skip school and continue sneaking out, I'm going to have to belt you. Is that understood?"

Jesse answered, "Yes, sir," but he continued skipping school and sneaking out, so that dreadful night came when Pat whipped off his belt after retrieving him from the park. Jesse just stood there with an "Oomph" each time the belt welted him from Pat's mighty swing. After about three harsh wallops, Pat threw down the belt and went into the bathroom, I believe to throw up, leaving Jesse standing there. Jesse waited a few minutes then quietly walked down the steps and took off on his bike.

We were all beside ourselves when two days passed and no one could find him. We contacted the sheriff's department and filed a missing-person report after a week. No one knew where he was. Though Jesse resurfaced after two weeks. Pat was shaken for many more. Jesse had pedaled two days to reach Port Orange, south of Daytona Beach, where he met an old couple at an orange grove who took him in. They had lost a son Jesse's age and begged him to stay with them. They wanted to adopt him, but I believe his engines were calling, because he hopped on his bike again and pedaled two days to get back home, and Daddy took him in.

We continued to be worried about Jesse. He was still running away. Every time he'd have a conflict with Daddy, like being sternly lectured for throwing a rod in his truck or etc., he'd leave, and we would not know where he was. He was repeatedly being found and returned by the sheriff's deputies or local police. Daddy was afraid if he didn't do something, Jesse would end up in serious trouble. Daddy previously resisted allowing the authorities to send Jesse to reform school, but, when Jesse continued to run away, Daddy said, "Take him away. I can't do anything with him." So, not knowing the terrible reputation they had for beating and torturing boys, he let them send him to Florida's School for Boys in Mariana. Many boys were sent there for truancy, running away, and even incorrigibility, including smoking cigarettes, along with much more egregious behavior.

When Jesse arrived in the Panhandle's juvenile reform institution, once the largest in the United States, he was shown around the South Side, or "Number 1" side of the massive 1,400-acre campus where the whites worked and lived. The North Side, or "Number 2," was for the blacks. Much of his memories of that time is scanty; however, he well remembers knowing from the get-go that it wasn't going to be an easy place to be. He was assigned to cottage 6 and thinks there were forty to fifty cottages.

When I asked him to relate what he *did* remember, he recalled, "Well, I remember when I first got there, I heard about the 'ice cream parlor,' also called the White House, where you could get the life beat out of you if you misbehaved or crossed with some of the guards. We were told we would be assigned an area to work in—you worked one day and went to school the next. I wanted to pick mechanics, but something happened to make me change my mind. I was in the canteen, and the lady who ran the sewing shop that was above the canteen was there. When she heard someone call me Meeks, she came over and asked, 'Are you possibly kin to Urbie Meeks?' When I told her he was my daddy, she pulled my shirt sleeve and said, 'I'm Dora. I knew your daddy, and you're coming to work with me.' I was always told I looked just like him when he was younger. I believe she had either dated him or knew him well in the past Somehow. He grew up in the Panhandle area. I remembered something Daddy always said, 'It's not what you know, but who you know.' I sensed I would need to know somebody in that place.

"I sewed dozens of the white gowns that the boys had to sleep in, and other things, plus we did all the upholstering of chairs and couches. That's how I learned to sew the canvas to rebuild my Sababra airplane and upholster the cars I refurbish. I joined the boxing team where we ran two miles every other day. I spent lots of time doing schoolwork and advanced three grades in school by working through three two-hundred units. I kept my nose clean and managed to navigate the rough waters. It was sure good to see family when they let me visit Bright Eyes when she came to see me during of her choir trips, but I was never so happy to see Daddy than when you, Pat, and he came to take me home after being there ten months."

We had a family gathering at Daddy's upon Jesse's return. Robert and Mack roasted a pig on coals in a hole in the backyard. They had the coals just right and the pig cooking since the wee hours of the morning before we left to bring Jesse home. We were so happy to have Jesse home, but seeing the way he walked around the place, patting the fender of the dump truck, walking around Mack's jalopies, nodding his head, and smiling, we knew who was happiest that he was back. Bo built a big bonfire, Robert cooked a huge pot of black-eyed peas, the girls baked cornbread, and all of us brought dishes of food and desserts. By dark, the family and many friends were feasting around the fire, singing, and exchanging tales, celebrating the return of Daddy's prodigal son.

Knowing now about the extreme physical and sexual abuse that existed at the very time Jesse was at the Mariana School for Boys, I was horrified to learn of the horrendous atrocities suffered by boys who were at the school when Jesse was. A website, WhiteHouseBoys. org, was formed by a former inmate for other inmates to share their stories about their experiences there. Most of their stories are too painful and horrific to believe. That the boys survived the beatings and abuse reported by many was nothing short of a miracle. I know that Mama was watching over Jesse, as was Daddy's long-lost friend Dora.

Bright Eyes & Buzz

Jesse, age 14

Chapter 21

The true meaning of life is to plant trees, under whose shade you do not expect to sit.

—Nelson Henderson

I didn't go into labor until a week before my due date in July. The morning before the fourth was a beastly hot day. I had just returned from my checkup when the pains started. I called Dink to say, "I think I'm having labor pains," and she was leaping up the steps and in my door within minutes. I had called Dr. Rowe, who said, "Check into St. Mary's, and I'll see you there." With no air conditioner or fans, I was soaked in perspiration. As I started to pull my smock over my head to take a shower, Dink said in a panicked voice, as she was stuffing my things into a bag, "You're not having that baby in the shower. Let's get you in the car right now." We dashed in the drenching rain holding newspaper over our heads to her little Hillman convertible parked downstairs. She ran upon sidewalks and around cars as water dripped into my lap from the leaky roof. I insisted we pull into a filling station to call Pat, who was working twenty miles south in Delray. He would have to find a way home. She had left her purse in my apartment and didn't have change to call, so she borrowed a couple of dimes from the gas attendant. When we arrived at the emergency room, we looked like drowned rats.

By the time a healthy John Patrick Jr. was born at five thirty-two that afternoon, the hall outside the delivery room was bustling with all of Pat's family and mine. His dad, normally very reserved, whizzed himself in a wheelchair up and down the hall. When Dr. Rowe brought the baby out for Pat to see, he couldn't get within a country mile of him for all my sisters.

186

When Johnny (Pat, Jr.) was a year old, we moved to a nice little house on a small lake—after we found a scorpion in Pat's work boot. Bobby Jean and Lulu often spent weekends with us and babysat occasionally. Jesse spent all his time working on cars, and all Bo wanted to do was to take care of the rabbits they were raising and go fishing with his dog, Buffus. The years were flying by and the kids were growing up fast.

Evelyn had moved to Tallahassee and married Abner. Coach and Dink adopted a baby boy and named him Rodney, and within a few years, Dink, Lois, Evelyn, and I had seven sons between us. Dink and Coach adopted a daughter, then Lois and I each gave birth to a daughter in 1960. The Meeks clan was increasing rapidly.

We were still taking turns helping the kids with various things and checking on Daddy, who continued to be up and down with health issues. He was still hauling dirt and opening his produce stand on his better days. Bobby Jean and Lulu drove with him when he went to North Florida and Georgia to buy pecans, peaches, and watermelon to sell. I don't believe he ever made a profit, because he always gave most of what he bought to needy neighbors and us girls for our families. He would pull up in front of our houses and say to our kids and the neighbors' kids, "Climb up in there and pick out the watermelon you want." Sometimes, he'd have six or eight kids climbing around melons in the back of his truck. He always kept us informed about what was being processed in the Belle Glade packing houses. He'd call us girls to say, "I'm in Belle Glade, and the beans or corn or tomatoes are being run in *such and such* packing house today. You better get out here and get those culls before they haul them off." Dink, Lois, and I would take turns babysitting all the kids while the other two would meet Daddy at the packing house. We would fill Lois's station wagon to the brim with seconds of whatever they were running that day. The next day or two, we'd get together and can whatever we had gotten or blanch it for our freezers. We spent days and weeks working together, babysitting, canning, painting, making drapes, upholstering, etc. that helped stretch budgets and made good memories. We'd get guavas that grew profusely along the road to the

Glades to make jelly, bananas along the canal banks, and mangos that grew along many roadsides in town.

*****

By the time we had our third son, James Patrick, I was determined to find a way for Pat and me to have our own home. I took real estate classes, read books, and learned about sweat equity. My brother Robert said, "I know of a partially built house where the deal fell through, and these builders just may consider this 'sweat equity' you talked about. When he took me to meet the builders and I saw the CBS structure with no interior walls or windows, I felt that house had to be ours. Miraculously, after a few visits and convincing, I suppose I talked enough real estate jargon to convince the builders to consider allowing us to do the plumbing, painting, landscaping, installation of cabinets, and enclose screens to back porch to create equity for our down payment. The builder said, "If your credit is good, and your husband thinks he can keep up with the other subs, we'll sign a contract. You must understand, if you fall behind, you lose your hard work."

The following week, we were taking the three boys to the building site after supper. They played underfoot while we scurried to keep up with the various stages of construction. At dusk we put all three boys in a playpen, secured it with netting to keep the thick swarms of mosquitos at bay, and worked until midnight or later. Somehow, we managed to keep up and complete our end of the bargain.

We borrowed five hundred dollars from Mom and Dad to purchase bathroom fixtures and needed materials, and with credit for sweat equity, we only had to come up with $142 for closing on September 19, 1959. Our new home was located a half block from the shores of Lake Osborne where Pat and I waterskied, had picnics, and dreamed of owning our own home. By Pat working side jobs on weekends and my budgeting, we paid Mom and Dad back the loan, plus interest we insisted on paying, by the end of that year. When I first discussed my plan with Daddy about getting our house, he said,

"Well, you know what Muhammad Ali says, 'If your mind can conceive it and your heart can believe it, you can achieve it.'"

We had barely moved into our new home when Pat was transferred to Daytona to finish a big school construction job. He rented a room in a boarding house and drove home to West Palm Beach every weekend. After a few weeks, I insisted on us taking the kids and joining him in Daytona. We could hardly pay our mortgages on our new home, but I wanted Pat to come home to his family nights. We rented an old house trailer in a run-down trailer park. I would take the kids to the beach most mornings to play in the sand and water's edge. I was expecting our fifth baby in less than a month.

Two years earlier, Lois married George Quick, who managed a nightclub in Palm Beach, with a partner and the umbrella and beach chair rentals on the beach of the Ambassador Hotel where she worked as a waitress. George also had partnered with Daddy in the dirt- and rock-hauling business. As we approached our house on Lakeview Drive, two huge piles of the blackest dirt I've ever seen—Daddy's black gold from the Glades—blocked our driveway. I knew we'd be hearing from George. He was always complaining in a teasing way that "the old man" gave all their profits away. Their partnership ended after Jesse backed one of their dump trucks too close to the edge of the water-filled sand pit and it slid in.

Beside the pile of muck was a huge citrus tree in a big plastic planter tub.

Daddy had been quite sick, so I was surprised when he drove up early the next morning in his truck with watermelons and several shovels in the back. I met him as he stepped from the truck. He said, "I brought the young'uns some fruit, but that there," pointing to the tree in the tub, "is a tangerine tree that will bring them fruit long after I'm gone, if we plant it right."

I felt sorry for Pat, because he had worked late every day last week so he could spend a restful weekend at home. I remembered how Daddy planted his fruit trees in Belle Glade, and we had to help him dig to plant them. Pat was in for some real digging.

As Daddy instructed, Pat dug a hole four feet deep with a six-foot diameter without questioning or complaining. With a couple of neighbors' help, they planted the tangerine tree. That tangerine tree was loaded every year, and the kids in the neighborhood knew they were stockholders having equal shares with the Rafter kids.

Jesse was now sixteen and a pretty good mechanic. He built his first race car from auto parts at Arant's junkyard. It was the first of many, painted blue with the number eight on each side and on the hood. We all gathered at the Palm Beach Raceway to watch his first race and gave him a standing ovation when he came in second. There was no stopping him from racing cars from Florida to Kokomo, Indiana. He had found his niche, and Daddy gladly shared some of his prohibition expertise in making his race car go faster. Bobby Jean and Lulu were still entertaining as a duet and becoming pretty good musicians.

Bobby Jean and Lulu were living with Dolly and Jake again, since Daddy had become sick. As soon as we got halfway settled in our new home, Bobby Jean came to live with us and share a room with our new daughter, Patti. At the same time, Coach and Mary Lou moved into a huge two-story home they purchased and renovated near the Intracoastal in the south end of town, and Lulu went to live with them and share a bedroom with their newly adopted baby girl, Karen. Bo and Jesse continued to stay with Daddy and Mack. Lulu would move from Dink to Lois and back to Daddy's from time to time. Bobby Jean remained with us for the next four years until Daddy became very sick near the end of her senior year of high school. He became bedridden and refused to stay in the hospital, so Barbara and Lulu moved back to Daddy's to care for him.

Daddy told Bobby Jean he would join us in celebrating her graduation but would skip the services. She said, "Well, I just won't walk in the procession in a gown. It's too expensive."

Daddy said, "No, you gotta walk down there and be proud of your accomplishment," but she said she would not do the procession bit.

Daddy said, "Okay, I will go, 'cause I want you to be proud about what you have done. I gave Buzz the money to buy what you need."

So Bobby Jean walked with her class and got about the loudest applause with the whole family there to see her accept her diploma. You'd think it was from Harvard.

We celebrated afterward at the Under 21 Club, where Shirley sang and a recording of her singing "Blue Moon" was featured for sale. The cover of the recording read, "Teenage Darling, Shirley Meeks." We were so proud of the two of them. Daddy was sick that night but went along with us, and we all had a wonderful time.

Once Daddy was feeling better, Bobby Jean joined the Air Force, while Lulu remained to care for Daddy. She continued to chauffeur Daddy to North Florida and Georgia to get his fruit and watermelon, and he continued bringing most of it to us girls.

We began taking turns having annual Christmas parties in each other's homes. The dads took turns being Santa and came on various modes of transportation. Over the years Santa arrived at our family parties on riding lawn mowers, motorcycles, horses, a catamaran Hobie Cat sailboat, water skis, and the City of West Palm's fire truck (where a family member was a fireman). Family and friends would bring musical instruments and a wrapped gift for Santa to give to the children they brought. We sisters always prepared the food, until after we ran out of food one year when the party swelled to almost two hundred people. After that, we had every family bring a dish and moved the parties to Lois and George's ten-acre ranch in Jupiter, where they kept their horses and spent weekends. We would have a huge bonfire that almost every year brought the fire department around. Our parties continued, with more people coming each year, creating memories for our family, extended families, and many friends.

Bobby Jean & Lulu singing

Lulu & Bobby Jean, guitar/accordion

Lulu's record cover

Bobby Jean – Air Force

Bobby Jean joins the Air Force

Lulu goes pro

Chapter 22

Hell is yourself and the only redemption is when a person puts himself aside to feel deeply for another.

—Tennessee Williams

Five years passed, and Daddy was still hanging on…

Daddy normally would have dressed himself and escaped from Good Samaritan Hospital, but this time it was different. He knew if he disconnected the tubes and wires, he would expire. Besides, with a serious case of pneumonia and high fever, he was too weak to consider it. It was heartbreaking, seeing his pale-blue eyes looking at us like an injured, caged animal—too weak to fight. His doctor advised us to call the family.

All ten siblings crowded into the room with him. Bobby Jean got an emergency leave from the Air Force through the American Red Cross, and Robert, Mack, Jesse, and Bo, who were working on a big construction job in Daytona Beach, rushed home. Dink, Lois, Evelyn, Lulu, and I lived locally and had kept a twenty-four-hour watch for the past week. We all watched as he floated in and out of consciousness. There was another patient in the room, but the nurses didn't drop by very often to check on either of them.

Amazingly, by the time everyone arrived, Daddy was somewhat conscious and asking for "something to drink." Bo said, "I could sure use something too." Daddy seemed to realize we were in the room and was making an effort to focus. As we encircled his bed and talked to him, he opened his eyes and squinted, trying to comprehend what was going on. He muttered, "Sing…a song," and closed his eyes.

We looked at each other wide-eyed. Lulu leaned over and asked, "What song do you want to hear, Daddy?"

He didn't answer. I quietly closed the door to his room and whispered, "In the Garden," and we started singing in harmony. "I come to the garden alone, while the dew is still on the roses, and the voice I hear, falling on mine ear—the Son of God is call...ing..." It was one of his and Mama's favorites. When the song ended, he managed a weak smile, opened his eyes slowly, and stared at Dink. "You sure...look like...your Mama..." He seemed to be coming out of the fog. We were soon doing what we learned from Mama—to talk about funny incidents to defuse our fear. I said, "Daddy, do you remember that summer we left Bo at a filling station in Indiana, and we suddenly realized the little bowlegged kid chasing Mule Train was Bo?" We all laughed, and he smiled. Bright Eyes added, "Daddy, do you know many jillion hours you sat outside movie theaters or at concession stands, reading newspapers, while we watched movies?" As usual, we continued feeding off each other, and Daddy perked up as he always did when we were all together. He mumbled, "You boys need to get back to work. Don't...be late." He closed his eyes, and his head slumped back onto the pillow. Dink quickly called the nurse, who checked his vitals and assured us, "His last pain shot kicked in, and he's just snoozing."

The boys parted with hugs and "drive safe" instructions from us girls, unaware that visit would be the last time they would hear Daddy tell them to stay on their game. Everyone went home except Bobby Jean and Lulu, who would man the nightshift.

The guys reported to the job Robert was supervising early the next morning. I know Mama was looking down and loving that they were working together. Our brothers and Verna's son Sonny had stayed close and worked mostly on the same construction sites, since Robert returned from the service and Jesse and Bo were old enough to work. They all had great work ethics and could always get a job, except our youngest brother, Bo. Sadly, he didn't seem to inherit that gene, but they covered for him. Though Bo and Robert drank too much, they also escaped the gene of Daddy's abusive behavior. Like Daddy, no matter how much Robert drank the night before, he was always the first—and the best—carpenter on the job. Although I'm sure there were always things that Mama would want to be different, I know she was still proud of her boys.

Daddy seemed to get better after his infusion of family, but he was still running a high fever and in serious condition. He didn't like being in Good Samaritan Hospital at the "Beach," as he called West Palm Beach and towns on the coast. He complained, "The doctors don't tell you anything. They treat you like mushrooms, keep you in the dark, and feed you bullshit." Uncle Vester told us he thought Daddy would get better care in Belle Glade Hospital where everybody knew him. That created a challenge for us older siblings who remembered what happened there sixteen years earlier when Mama died. Daddy *did* know more people and had more clout in 1964 than Mama had in 1948, so we squelched our negative thinking and agreed to have him moved. We thought Mama would want us to. Uncle Vester and Verna paid an ambulance to transport him to his beloved "Muck," as he called the Glades.

We girls took turns, two at a time, driving the fifty-six miles to Belle Glade General Hospital daily, where Uncle John's daughter, Bonnie, was a nurse.

Bobby Jean and Lulu went to Daytona to visit the guys and celebrate Lulu's eighteenth birthday in July, because the guys couldn't take time off to come home.

One afternoon, when it was Dink's and my turn to check on Daddy, flashing red lights lit up the hall a few doors from his room, and a loud voice came from speakers overhead, "Code Blue, room 202, code blue in 202!" Oh my gosh, that was Daddy's room number. We started in a run but stopped and backed against the wall when a stream of nurses and staff with machines scurried past us to Daddy's room. A nurse told us we should wait in the alcove down the hall. We waited, and another nurse informed us he had another heart attack, but they had him stabilized and needed a bit longer before we could see him. It was eleven o'clock that night before they finally let us see him. I thought of what Uncle Vester said after Daddy's sixth or seventh trip to the hospital over the years, "Urbie is like a cat that has nine lives, but he's just about used up all of them." At the rate he was going, I prayed he still had a few left.

Daddy was heavily sedated, and we sat in chairs against the window and whispered quietly. We didn't engage in conversation with him because we wanted him to rest. He had wires and tubes attaching him to machines, making all kinds of noises. He was making strange, muffled noises as well and seemed to be hallucinating. I don't want to remember seeing him like that, but I will never forget what happened that night.

Out of the blue, Daddy raised his head and called Dink's name loud and clear. We both jumped up and rushed to his bedside. He tried to reach out to her, and as she grasped his hand, he looked up and said, "You…did good…Dink." His head flopped back onto the pillow, and his eyes closed. He was exhausted, but he seemed to be breathing better since he came to Belle Glade.

Dink was too choked up to say anything. She held his hand and brushed his cheek, as tears tumbled down hers. Overwhelmed, she collapsed onto the edge of the bed and sobbed a hardly audible, "Th…ank you, Daddy."

Not knowing what to do, I stood close to Dink and rubbed her shoulders gently until the sobbing subsided. When she leaned over and kissed Daddy on the cheek, I knew she had finally forgiven Daddy, as Mama wanted us all to do.

We stayed until midnight before driving back to West Palm Beach, completely whipped, but thankful he had survived another episode.

Daddy's health had been touch-and-go for several years now. We knew he was "worn out" as we'd hear him say, but when we'd tell him he was trying to do too much, he'd say, "It's better to wear out than rust out." He was not one to give up. We knew he was hanging on to see "all his young'uns grow up," but it was hard watching him suffer.

The next time my turn came around was a week later with Bobby Jean. She had gotten an honorable discharge from the Air Force with a favorable record to help care for Daddy. He hadn't recognized any of us the past week. As Bobby Jean and I stayed by his bed, I sensed from his short, shallow breathing that this just might be his ninth encounter with luck. We stood there, looking for a sign of cognizance, when he barely opened his eyes and whispered, "I'...m so...ti...red. All...gr...own. Go see...John...ny down... hall." We realized he was talking about Uncle John, his brother, who had recently died in the same hospital. We put our ear closer as he was trying to talk. In a barely audible voice, he said, "Shor...ty," and bells and whistles went off on all the machines and the nurses came running. We stepped back to allow the nurses by his bed. When the machines went silent and they turned to us with an expression of sincere sympathy, we knew he was gone.

Covering her mouth and sinking to the floor, Bobby Jean screamed hysterically, and for once, I couldn't seem to quiet her. I wanted to scream too, but I knew I had to stay calm and soothe her fears, as Mama had done for us so many times. I hugged her tight and tried to think of something to alleviate our pain, but my mind went blank. I finally was able to croak, "He was in pain, Bobby Jean...He said he was tired, and...he will be with Mama and our baby sister now."

*****

Everyone came home again for Daddy's funeral. He had accomplished his goal and died in peace at age seventy-six, on September 18, 1964, knowing our youngest, Lulu, had turned eighteen two months before. It may have been helter-skelter, but between Daddy, Dink, older siblings, other good angels, and God's watchful eye, the ten surviving siblings were finally old enough to be on our own and still all together as Mama wanted.

We knew he didn't want a church service, but we recruited a lay pastor to say some prayers for his soul, just in case. The big room at Quattlebalm's Funeral Home was packed with family, politicians, and friends, including Mother Pace, Nell Smith, Lake Lytle, and some kids from the home. Though I felt a tremendous sense of loss, I was also feeling an esoteric sense of gratitude for all that had happened in our life that brought us to where we were, knowing that so many wonderful things in our lives would not have happened if the bad things had not happened. Thinking of this reaffirmed what Mama always said, "Everything always happens for a reason," and what Daddy said, in quoting Thoreau, "The years tell much that the days never show."

After they loaded the casket into the back of the long black car and we climbed into the one behind it, I felt a chilling déjà vu as we rolled through the wrought iron gates at Woodlawn Cemetery. We wound through narrow paths to the same gravesite where we'd gathered sixteen years before. The scene was the same and brought chills—the tent with chairs lined up on artificial green turf, the black velvet–draped stand over a hole in the ground—but something was different. It must have been an omen for good things to come. The black velvet stayed in place, hiding the cold steel on the metal stand, the sun was blazing, and there wasn't a cloud in the sky.

After we sang "Amazing Grace" and listened to the pastor's last words, family and friends meandered slowly down the narrow paths and out the wrought iron gates, except us siblings. We stood together under the canopy, sharing memories, prolonging our last goodbye to Daddy. Jesse said, "When Daddy whipped my butt for throwing a rod in the dump truck, and he had a job to deliver—and when Pat beat my butt—I know it hurt them more than it hurt me."

I said, "I can't believe someone finally got him inside a church, but we couldn't do that to him now, but I sure would like to know why he didn't want to go into a church."

Mack said, "Well, you know how he hated hypocrites, liars, and cheaters. I guess, since he declared preachers who bought his moonshine hypocrites, he figured if he went inside a church, he would be a hypocrite too. Who knows? Daddy was a complicated man."

Bo added, "But Daddy was a good man."

As we were chatting, two men approached the casket on the velvet-draped stand over the hole in the ground. We huddled around the stand with arms around each other's waist. The men began to lower Daddy into the ground next to Mama. Blinded by tears, I prayed in silence, "Dear God, I am not sure if Daddy's effort to keep us together was enough to redeem his sins and allow him into heaven. I pray it was! But I am sure it was enough to keep us kids from growing up in a living hell. Please be merciful. Mama would want you to be—and so do we."

The tombstone off to the side read "Urbie E. Meeks, 1889–1964" and "Myrtle Leila Meeks & Inf, 1909–1948."

Ring the bells that still can ring, forget the perfect offering. There is a crack in everything, that's how the light gets in.

—Leonard Cohen

Epilogue

After Daddy…

There were twists, turns, and high hurdles to jump for some along the road to success, but we all stuck together and usually found a way to laugh or sing away problems. We made a fun adventure out of the challenges that faced any of our clan and filled the broken cracks with value.

Before Daddy passed, Robert had remarried and had another daughter and a son. Soon after Daddy died, he was divorced. After brief marriages, Jesse and Bo were divorced too. Robert took a job supervising construction in Alaska for a new start. Mack and Jesse went with him and opened J&M Roofing Company in Anchorage. Bo tagged along to work with them, and Bobby Jean joined them to cook and keep house. They rented a big home, where they all lived together. Lulu, distressed over Daddy's death, disappeared for a year,  but she reappeared and joined them in Alaska after stints of singing on cruise ships and wing walking in Bill Adams' air show. She became a very popular entertainer singing in Alaska.

Bobby Jean and Lulu met their husbands in Alaska, and each had three children. After living in the north land for many years, Lulu divorced and took her kids to Florida. Bobby Jean and her family ended up in Phoenix, Arizona, where she stayed, after she and her husband agreed to disagree about the kids doing hip-hop. She and Lulu would join forces off and on as single moms. They raised the most good-hearted, hard-working, and successful kids ever. Did I mention that we all have great kids and grandkids? Many of them are talented musicians: Lulu's kids and grandkids have beautiful voices and play the guitar; Bobby Jean's Joe and Jesse have toured the United States and Japan as the popular hip-hop "Phunk Junkees"; Bright Eye's granddaughter Tylre plays the banjo; our grandson Kazem is an accomplished violinist and plays the mandolin; Lois's Gigi has a beautiful voice and plays the piano; Robert's son Bobby is a professional country singer; and Dink's Karen has a beautiful voice. We attend a lot of performances, and family gatherings always include a lot of music.

Jesse married a single mom with three kids, and J&M Roofing was flourishing. We were devastated when Mack slipped from an icy, high-pitched roof. When he died a week after the accident. Jesse closed J&M Roofing and moved his family from Anchorage to Kenai. He became a mechanic at Homer Electric and threw himself into building race cars and john boats. He got his pilot's license and refurbished an airplane. Once the kids grew up, he retired from Homer Electric, and he and Mary retired in Missouri. Before they retired, he had to get a special item off his bucket list—he rode his motorcycle across the Alcan Highway from Alaska to South Florida and back to Alaska. He built a workshop bigger than his home, where he still refurbishes old automobiles at age 74. Our youngest and oldest brothers, Bo and Robert had heart problems from an early age, and, sadly, we also lost them both way too soon to heart failure.

After Bright Eyes and Abner parted ways, she got her degree and worked with special needs students and became involved with Special Olympics. As plumbers, teachers, waitresses, electricians, geologist, and about any career or job title you can name, I like to think of our family, like most, as an asset to society. Bright Eyes' family is involved with NVC, non-violent-communication, and working with and teaching undeveloped countries subsistence skills, they make a massive contribution for creating a better world. After Bright Eyes lost her husband, she bought a home in Tallahassee, where family travelers pause for a stopover between Arizona, Missouri, and Georgia when visiting family in South Florida.

Lois, George, and his business partner managed the restaurant and bar, the Olympus, at the Palm Beach International Airport and the concessions at the Palm Beach Raceway and Palm Beach Auditorium. She made slinky royal blue satin gowns with Greek Key trim for the hostesses and waitresses and vests for the waiters and bar tenders. She became a black belt karate instructor and taught classes at the YMCA. 1975, she moved to Alaska with her three kids and dog, divorced George, and joined the ranks of single moms. After meeting a bush pilot, she learned to fly, bought an airplane, and eighty acres of land in Alaska. She fell in love with the bush pilot, but not with Alaska. They got married with the agreement they would both retire and spend winter in Florida and summers in Alaska. Sometimes we make promises we can't keep—she hated the cold winters and he just couldn't leave his Alaska. It was sad she was in Florida when his plane went down while he was flying supplies for the Iditarod dog sled races from Anchorage to Nome. She remained in Florida, became a massage therapist and retired on her ten-acre ranch in Jupiter. Marshal was a great guy who will always be loved and missed.

Dink and Coach bought a forty–nine–acre farm in Franklin, North Carolina with a garnet and ruby mine. He taught school and they ran the mine in the summer. The seven male cousins spent summers at Aunt Dink's farm. They bunked together in the barn, rode Rodney's donkey, dug dirt to be mined, and wandered around the hills of Carolina. "Aunt Dink" wouldn't let them eat if they didn't write a letter once a week to their parents. The cousins have wonderful, life-long memories of summers there. After the kids grew up, Dink and Coach retired on a big, luxury fishing boat on the intracoastal waterway in Jupiter, Florida. After Coach died, she took up painting and became a talented painter and designer of jewelry. She lives at the Moose Haven retirement community near Jacksonville where she still paints and keeps the place jumping at age ninety-one.

I didn't try to write the story of our half-siblings, George, Luvera, Ithaniel, Verna, and Nelly, because that's their children's story to tell.

Pat and I went to Alaska in 1975 with our five kids for a one-year adventure that ended up being four. When we returned to Florida, two of our sons and daughter stayed. Pat loved Alaska and I believe he wanted to stay, but I convinced him we should get back to our rental properties—and sunshine. We returned to West Palm Beach, where Pat set up and supervised a pre-fab shop for a mechanical contractor and taught plumbing apprenticeship classes two nights a week. I held licenses as a real estate broker, appraiser, and mortgage broker, so I worked in various areas of real estate. We bought and renovated small homes to resale or keep for rental income. We built a small condo complex, Sunset Villas, that we retained and leased for retirement income. Alaska is an experience that calls you back. We returned for another four-year stint in 1981. We returned south and Pat retired after working ten years as the chief mechanical inspector for the city of West Palm Beach. We are happy in our downsized home in West Palm Beach, enjoying adventures with kids, grandkids, family and friends. Our sons married wonderful girls and raised their four kids in Alaska, giving us reason to return again and again for visits. Lulu ended up back in Alaska with her kids, where they raised their families and increased Alaska's population considerably.

I would be amiss if I didn't tell you that our huge clan include our share of those who inherited Daddy's addiction to alcohol. I am thankful and happy to say that most have won their battle, but sad to say that a couple didn't, and they are still in the ring slugging it out. But I'm sure, with the whole family piling on, they too will win in the end.

The seven surviving siblings are spread across the country, but we still manage to come together to celebrate special occasions: weddings, graduations, land-mark birthdays, special accomplishments, and to support each other when the support of the clan is needed. We always feel the presence of our parents as we keep them alive in our memories.

Mama (Leila)

Daddy 5th St. (Belle Glade) 1948

6 sisters

Dink at Moose Haven

Jesse with Mary

Pat _ Betty developed rental proterties, growing old together

Betty M. Rafter (Buzz) and her husband, Patrick, live in Florida. If they're not on the Alcan Highway en route to visit family in Alaska, or wandering somewhere out west in their travel trailer, they can be found at home reading, writing, or planning their next adventure. Like Betty's daddy told her and her siblings, "You should always have something to look forward to and something to look back on."

CPSIA information can be obtained
at www.ICGtesting.com
Printed in the USA
BVHW030250180919
558691BV00001B/1/P